Blog Prompts

101 Creative Topics that Attract Customers, Invite Discussion and Help You Create a Loyal Legion of Fans

Sherice Jacob

Blog Prompts: 101 Creative Topics that Attract Customers, Invite Discussion and Help You Create a Loyal Legion of Fans

Copyright © 2015 by Sherice Jacob

Acknowledgements

Special thanks go out first and foremost to my family. Everything I've done and everything I've become has been possible because of your love and support!

I'd also like to thank the bloggers and entrepreneurs I work with and meet each and every day, for their suggestions, ideas and improvements. This book was written for, and because of – you!

Table of Contents

Chapter 1: What Makes a Successful Blog? 14

Chapter 2: Sharing Your Knowledge 18

Chapter 3: Working Together with Other Bloggers 46

Chapter 4: The Simple Things 72

Chapter 5: Changes and Shifts 103

Introduction

Have you ever wondered what truly makes a blog? Why is it that some blogs enjoy an almost-instant surge in popularity (and money) and others seem to wither on the vine?
It all boils down to three simple words:

"Content is KING!"

That has been the rallying cry of online marketers, A-list bloggers and brand specialists for years now. If you create helpful, informative, interesting or unique content – they will come.

But they've left out a critical piece of the puzzle.

How, exactly, are you supposed to create this riveting content if every other blogger in your same field has already covered the basics? There's already plenty of scraped, spun, salvaged and rehashed content out there.

You want your blog to be different: to stand out and get noticed for its thought-provoking, incredibly-helpful (and maybe even debate-sparking!) posts.

You're ready to grab your readers by the (eye)balls and make them recognize that you're well on your way to becoming an authority in your field.

That's where Blog Prompts can help.

Developed by Sherice Jacob, a blogger with over 10 years of experience in niche marketing and online copywriting, Blog Prompts was created with a simple promise: to give you the creative jolt you need to write thoughtful, inspiring, motivating and controversial posts that cement your blog's place among the experts.

How to Use This Book

To get started, simply flip through the pages until you find an idea that piques your curiosity. Blog Prompts isn't meant to be read from cover to cover – rather it's designed to give you that spark of inspiration and momentum you need in a pinch, when "blogger's block" has set in.

Each chapter is divided into broad areas that are based on the tone you want your writing to take. Do you prefer working with other bloggers? Chapter 3 is all about posts that invite collaboration. Looking for tools and services to help you become a more professional blogger? Chapter 5 has you covered.

Getting Straight to the Good Stuff

Blog Prompts already assumes that you know what a blog is, and have set one up – either on your own website or through a third-party service like Blogger.com or Wordpress.com. That isn't to say that you won't get any help from this book making sure your content gets into the hands (or screens) of your readers. Be sure to visit blogprompts.com for the latest topics, creativity-building exercises and everything you need to help your blog become a success. Good luck!

Chapter 1: What Makes a Successful Blog?

In all my years of blogging and helping to write and design blogs for others, I've seen many of them evolve into incredible resources for their readers. I've also seen blogs that never truly connected with their audience and seemed to go full steam ahead in the wrong direction.

The difference wasn't in the design, the chosen topic or the blogger, although those parts do play a role. The closer I looked, the more I noticed that successful blogs seemed to follow an unspoken set of rules. These "best practices" work with any subject, for any person, with no technical know-how needed whatsoever. They are:

Rule #1: Be Observant

Watch and learn. Great writers and marketers have done it for hundreds of years – and great bloggers do it today. They subscribe to their favorite blogs, get alerts on new trends, reach out through social networks and generally keep their finger on the ever-humming pulses of the blogosphere and social networks. They see what's working for others and they adapt it for themselves.

That's not to say you should copy, plagiarize or steal. Your own experiences, perspective and ideas can help make the post your own. **It's not being lazy – it's being smart.** And it's necessary for Rule #2…

Rule #2: Find a Shortcut

As you keep blogging and more people come to seek out your expertise and opinion – **you will get busy**. And yet as your time starts to shrink and you become a more in-demand authority on your topic, you'll still be expected to churn out those killer posts that everyone is waiting for.

You need a shortcut.

Beyond being observant, you should also note any blogs whose headlines or story angles interest you. It doesn't matter if they're in the same industry or on the same topic as yours. What matters is that they promised a benefit or a story so good, you just had to click.

Save these tidbits for later. Write them down or copy and paste them into a file on your computer. Use your favorite smart phone app or web-based service. Whatever is most comfortable for your record-keeping needs and lets you access them from anywhere.

Direct sales marketers and copywriters call it a "swipe file" – and it's exactly what it sounds like. They "swipe" headlines and pieces of other sales letters, and file them away for future reference. That way, they don't have to wrack their brains trying to come up with the perfect pitch when the next big project lands on their desk, and the deadline is yesterday.

Which leads me to the third rule…

Rule #3: Don't Beat Yourself Up

As a proficient writer who has worked with everyone from business startups to well-known corporate brands, I will tell you that not every post you write is going to hit it out of the park. And it's not because you're not smart enough, not tech-savvy enough or aren't working hard enough. Some blog posts completely backfire, are misread and misunderstood, and tend to take on a life of their own. Sometimes you might say something, hit "publish", and immediately regret it.

Don't beat yourself up. You're only human. Your blog is only a collection of 1's and 0's. People might disagree with you – to the point where it seems like they're digitally frothing at the mouth. Others might stand with you, building on what you've written and adding their own points of view. Some may even go out and start their own blogs because of something you said. Good. That's the way it should be. Blogs evolve, people change and you have the right to an opinion.

Rule #4: Go the Extra Mile (But Don't Reveal the Destination!)

It might seem like extra work to do the research, find the case studies, gather the screenshots and show the proof in your posts. But this extra work will pay off because most people don't want to go the extra mile. They think it's too much work or too time-consuming, so they'll link to you instead.

As you get more links from other sites, word starts to spread and more people learn about and link to your post. Pretty soon, you'll become known as the go-to resource for that topic. Congratulations – you've just created your first piece of cornerstone content!

What is Cornerstone Content?

It's known by other names too – like flagship content or evergreen content. Basically, it's content that's so thorough, helpful and actionable, people can't help but refer to it time and time again. Great cornerstone content can even last for years without much of an update. And the blogs which have taken the time to develop it are more successful than those who haven't.

But that's not to say you should pour out every ounce of knowledge in your posts. Otherwise, you may find that people aren't commenting because there's nothing left for them to add. By "not revealing the destination", you're making a statement or asking a question, then stepping back and letting your audience chip in with their two cents.

Rule #5 - Make it Unique by Making it Yours

Just because "it's been done before" doesn't mean it's finished. Even well-known magazines run what seem like almost identical articles month after month, and you don't see fiery letters to the editor complaining about it. Great posts startle our curiosity. They include enough of a teaser in the headline to make us wonder "what *else* am I missing?" And if done right, the post leaves you satisfied but still hungry for more.

To transform a blog prompt into a real spark, you've got to take all the passion – all the things you love about your topic, all the things you hate, all of your experiences and everything in between, and share it in such a way that you just know each and every reader is going to get real value out of it.

Keep reminding yourself that there will never be a better time to write that post – and that everyone who reads it is going to come away more motivated, inspired or educated.

Let's get started!

Chapter 2: Sharing Your Knowledge

This chapter is all about posts which invite you to be yourself while inviting discussion from others. If you think the blogosphere is crowded as it is, remember that there's no one else like you out there. No one has your unique experiences, skill-set, tone or writing style. Your writing could be someone else's "light bulb moment" – that point at which they finally "get it", even after reading lots of other blogs or websites.

Just don't try to be something (or someone) you're not. When you do, you're leaving far too many of your best qualities behind. If you're more comfortable using a pen name, or even taking a pseudonym of the opposite gender – that's fine too. Do whatever makes you feel comfortable enough to move forward with confidence.

That "moving forward" part is what makes the difference.

Introduce Yourself

Although your blog readers can't shake your hand, read your body language or infer your mood from the tone of your voice, your writing says a lot about you as a person. Your first post is a great opportunity to introduce yourself – or if you've already started blogging, take the time to share a bit more of your personality with your readers. Who are you, really?

- Why do you blog? What inspired you to set out on this particular path?

- Do you have a mentor who encouraged you or other inspirational moments where you knew you had to get out and share your perspective with others?

- How did you get involved in the industry, organization or topic you're writing about?

- Do you have a unique history? Experience? Awards?

- Tell us about your education, your life growing up or jobs you held and how they contributed (good or bad) and led you to the point you're at now.

People don't connect with blogs – they connect with other people. Strike a common ground with your reader. Talk about a few of your favorite things and invite others to do the same.

What Are You Grateful For?

It's pretty common (and some would say clichéd) to do this in the U.S. on or around the Thanksgiving holiday – but there's absolutely nothing wrong with that. You can do this on any day you like.

Make a Gratitude List – talk about the people, events and even the "little" things in life that make you thankful.

Still feeling stuck? Ponder on these points:

- Is there a song, movie or book that really changed the way you think or opened your mind?

- Did you have an amazing parent, teacher, friend or mentor who helped you become the person you are today?

- Were you given some incredible (or even awful) advice? Are you better off now that you acted on, or ignored it?

- How have different events in your life shaped the person you've become?

Make your list, even if the points on it aren't directly related to your business. Chances are, you'll touch on a point or two that your readers can really relate to. Don't forget to ask them to make their own lists and share them in the comments!

Write about a Trait You've Noticed that Makes You Like or Admire Someone

We all pay attention to other people – and there's often something about them that we wish we could develop in ourselves. What are those traits for you? What is it about them that makes you take notice and look up to that person?

It could be that you consider yourself a real dynamic go-getter, but you admire the quiet, self-assured brilliance of a fellow blogger or colleague who is more of an introvert. Perhaps you wish you could calm your impulsiveness and be more cautious.

Or maybe you're more introverted, and you watch (from the sidelines, of course!) all the creative eccentrics out there having fun and becoming more in-tune and comfortable with themselves. You listen, observe and make mental notes.

It doesn't matter what the particular trait is, or who the person is. It could be your next-door neighbor or a celebrity. Getting it out in the open is what matters. Invite your visitors to share their own likeable traits and the people they admire. You may be surprised at the different perspectives and points of view!

Make a Blogger's "Bucket List"

A "bucket list" is a list of things you want to do before you die. They could be as grandiose as skydiving or as simple as planting a tree.

A blogger's "Bucket List" is a list of things you'd like to do through your blog, within the timeframe you set. Set goals for your bucket list for anywhere from a month to a year (or several!) down the road – then set about achieving them.

Some ideas to help you get started:

- Guest blog for a popular blogger in your niche.

- Get featured in a major magazine/newspaper.

- Get interviewed or featured on TV.

- Take part in an important conference or workshop in your industry and then blog about your experience.

- Win an award specific to your topic (such as a Top Blog for Writers, Best Mom Blogger Award, etc.)

- Get an authority in your niche to guest post and share their expertise.

- Create a course that walks people through the process you blog about.

- Write a book detailing your blogging experience. What's worked? What hasn't? What do you wish you'd done differently?

Think big and dream bigger. It doesn't matter if the goal seems impossible now. Type it out and then hit publish. Ignore the naysayers and critics if there are any. Once your goals are out in the open, you'll be surprised at how the universe "conspires" to make them happen for you.

Of course, you have to make a plan and work toward them as well, otherwise you'll get caught up in the blizzard of day-to-day activities with nothing achieved. Start by contacting some of the top sites in your niche and ask about guest posting opportunities. Don't give up.

Take an Opposing Stance on a Trend that Everyone in Your Industry Loves or is Talking About

It could be a social network, an upcoming product or some other trending superstar. People just can't stop talking about it. Whether they're inflating it to larger-than-life status or your inbox is filled with a flurry of blog posts about it – whatever "it" is, write about its flaws or potential shortcomings.

This isn't to say that you should go on a ranting rampage or completely berate someone. No matter how much you may dislike "it", you have to expect that a lot of fans are going to come to "its" defense when you make your post – so do so constructively.

Comment on the pros, but focus on the cons.

Revealing the "man behind the curtain" will not only give your blog a different slant on a popular topic (and hence, more attention as opposed to the "me too" bloggers who are gushing about it), but it can also serve as a wake-up call to people following the trend that may only be getting one-sided advice about it.

Conversely, you could also highlight something (or someone) that you feel isn't getting enough attention. Perhaps they launched their site or product at the wrong time, or they feel like they're talking in an echo chamber – a little nudge could help nourish their soul and fuel their ambition.

What Are Some Books You Feel You Can't Possibly Live Without? Why Do You Enjoy Them So Much?

This post starts out like the famous "if you were on a desert island and could only take…" prompt, but can go so much deeper. Share your favorite reading list and why those particular books inspired you. What did you learn from them, and how did it impact your blog or your life?

You could actually separate this post into two separate branches if you liked – books that you enjoyed on a professional level (such as productivity/time management, boosting creativity, marketing, etc.) and books that you enjoyed in your specific niche.

To take this post idea one step further, you could turn it into a rich media publication by using two Amazon features – Listmania lists[1] and/or So You'd Like To…[2]

Both of these methods let you find and recommend your favorite books to other customers and earn a commission on the ones you sell. The "So You'd Like To…" option lets you share your expertise in your niche by helping others choose the best materials to learn from.

[1] How to Create a Listmania List:
http://www.amazon.com/gp/help/customer/display.html?nodeId=14279651

[2] Amazon's "So You'd Like To…" Guide
http://www.amazon.com/gp/richpub/syltguides/create?

The "Mix Tape" Blog Post

Right in line with the books post is the mix tape blog post. Tell us what songs are currently loaded into your iPod or mp3 player and how they make you feel.

This particular style of post is great for blogs that focus on somehow improving your life – weight loss, creativity exercises and productivity tips just to name a few. Lots of people search for playlists for throwing parties, exercising or just winding down after a long day.

The music we listen to is a highly personal choice, and some people (like me!) have such eclectic tastes that it's hard to pin down a playlist that pulls from one particular style. But music, books, and even movies can be great virtual ice-breakers and get your visitors more involved. They may even offer new suggestions you hadn't considered, or post their own lists in the comments.

Take a Famous Movie and Apply its Lessons or Story to Your Business

It could be something as simple as what *Marley and Me* can teach you about dog training, or as abstract as what *The Godfather* can teach you about gardening. You can really let your creative muse come out to play on this particular prompt.

It's a good idea to look through the top-grossing movies of all-time[3] to get some ideas on what's popular, and what many people have already seen, so that you'll be able to tie it in with your business or industry and spur comments from your readers.

I've seen posts about what *Abraham Lincoln: Vampire Hunter* can teach you about home remodeling, and what *Raiders of the Lost Ark* can teach women about fashion. So don't think your connection is too far-fetched to make sense! One thing is for certain – it will definitely get people talking.

[3] IMDB - All-Time Worldwide Box Office
http://www.imdb.com/boxoffice/alltimegross?region=world-wide

Should Everyone Have Your Product or Service? Why or Why Not?

Let's face it – not everyone is a good fit for your offer. Sometimes it may even be worth filtering your readers through a blog post. This is especially common for higher tier products where a greater level of expertise, work or time needs to be committed in order to succeed. Things that, quite honestly, not everyone has.

But before you think that I'm advising you to cut out a huge section of your customer base, you can always tweak this prompt to offer a "lite" or "basic" version of your offer to people who aren't quite ready to take the plunge, but are still interested in knowing how you can help them.

You should always, always have multiple products or services that you can offer your ideal customer along the way. Consider them like stepping stones along the path of progress.

Getting people to take action usually starts with "lots of little yes's" – offering small, helpful products or services at a low price point that act as a bridge to the next step up. This in turn builds momentum along the way toward the next offer or product. People who have already purchased from you once and had a good experience will be very likely to do so again.

Find a Common Issue that Many People Care About and Relate it to Your Blog

When Carole Sevilla Brown of EcoSystemGardening.com learned that the National Wildlife Federation (NWF) had teamed up with Scotts (the company behind Round-Up® weed killer and Miracle-Gro® among other things) she was understandably upset. Not only did she alert her readers to the seedy partnership, but it caused such a backlash that Scotts products were boycotted and donations to the NWF were slashed.

The furor was so great that NWF spokesman David Mizejewski tried to subdue the collateral damage by agreeing to let Carole interview him. Questions were collected from readers, but the interview turned out to be more of a corporate green-washing attempt than a serious opportunity to make amends and spark change.

Ultimately, NWF withdrew their partnership after accusations came to light that Scotts had to pay 4.5 million dollars in fines because of toxic chemicals in their birdseed. Carole's blog, her legion of fans and followers, and relationships with other like-minded bloggers brought the issue to the forefront of their discussions, and didn't let go. That's just one example of the sheer power of many voices versus one corporation.

What are some ways you can draw attention to a cause on your blog, and be the spark of change for the better?

Look Outside Your Industry for Inspiration

In the copycat world of blogging, once a particular style of post becomes popular, other blogs follow suit. All you have to do is look at the evergreen popularity of list posts ("5 Reasons to Own a Widget"), resource posts ("101 Free Widgets for Your Next Project") and tutorial posts ("How to Create Your Own Widget in 3 Easy Steps") to see this example at work.

Tired of the same old thing? Want to make your own posts stand out? Focus your attention away from what the herd is doing to see what's gaining traction in other industries. Here are some examples to spur your creativity:

- **The Manifesto Post** – Once reserved only for politics, the manifesto post aims to create a set of guidelines that others can aspire to follow.

- **The Crowdsourced Post** – Crowdsourcing is outsourcing a problem or task to a group of (often unidentified) people. This is a great method for getting feedback or input on a project-in-progress. Getting started is as simple as asking your audience, or going through a paid platform like IdeaScale.com

- **The "Laws"/"Rules" Post** – You don't have to turn the lessons you've learned into a general list post. Instead, turn them into laws, or rules – such as The Unbreakable Rules of Graphic Design or 10 Laws of Weatherproofing Your Home.

Share How You First Got Into the Industry/Niche that You're In

Almost everyone has an interesting story about how they got into the line of work they're currently doing. Why not share yours?

Don't forget to share the things you wish you would've known when you started out so that others can avoid the potential pitfalls and learn what to do and what not to do.

To take this idea one step further, you can write a post detailing how someone can get into your same line of work. Remember that people of all ages will likely be reading your blog, so you could elaborate on:

- Which classes/courses to take (and which ones to avoid).

- Which skills are the most in-demand.

- Common myths and misconceptions about your industry.

- What specific areas that beginners should focus on for best results.

- A timeline or checklist that outlines each step to take and when.

- Mistakes or missteps you made when first starting out, that you wish you'd known earlier.

Start a Blog-a-Thon and Donate a Portion of the Revenues of Any Products Purchased or Ads Clicked During that Time to a Good Cause

A blog-a-thon is a great way to raise money for a cause you're passionate about, while growing your website's traffic. It can be a group effort where you blog for a set number of hours straight, or you can work at it for a full 30 days. Whichever you choose, keep the following timeline in mind:

The Week Before...
- Discuss deadlines, headlines and topics with your fellow blog authors if you're working together as a group. Profile your fellow contributors and use social media to keep visitors informed about their posts.

- Start generating excitement about the blog-a-thon by profiling the charity you're donating to, what it means to you, and how long the event will be running.

The Day Before...
- Create profiles of your fellow authors and highlight their special offers with links back to their respective blogs.

- Include a simple calendar to keep visitors informed about upcoming posts.

During the Event...
- Use a social media scheduling service like HootSuite.com to schedule and announce posts. Give readers a cliff-hanger for the next post in the sequence.

- Do a weekly recap of posts along with some of the most interesting or engaging comments in the discussion.

After the Event...

- Compile the posts into a free e-book which visitors can download in exchange for a Facebook "Like", a Twitter tweet, or a donation to the charity you're supporting.

Adopt a Meme – a.k.a "Memejacking"

Memes are ideas or behaviors that spread quickly over the Internet. If you've been on the web for any length of time, you may recognize popular memes including "Success Kid", "Honey Badger" and "Y U No Guy" [4]. They're fun, creative, and clever.

If done carefully and appropriately, memes can be successfully used for marketing and promotional purposes too – a process called memejacking.

The most important thing to understand about memejacking is that it needs to be done early for best results. No one wants to be late to the popular meme party – so if you notice a popular graphic making the rounds on your Facebook page (where memes tend to spread), look for ways that you can apply it to your topic.

To learn more about this hidden marketing tactic, check out the Hubspot article "Memejacking: The Complete Guide to Creating Memes for Marketing" [5]. You can also create a graphic based on popular memes at **http://memegenerator.net**

[4] 10 Popular Memes Masquerading as Marketing Campaigns
http://blog.hubspot.com/blog/tabid/6307/bid/33197/10-Popular-Memes-Masquerading-as-Marketing-Campaigns.aspx

[5] Memejacking: The Complete Guide to Creating Memes for Marketing
http://blog.hubspot.com/blog/tabid/6307/bid/33363/Memejacking-The-Complete-Guide-to-Creating-Memes-for-Marketing.aspx

Put the Spotlight on Something in Your Industry that You Feel Doesn't Get the Attention It Deserves

Rather than taking an opposing stance on something everyone else is raving over, this prompt lets you highlight something that (in your opinion) has been sitting on the sidelines for far too long.

It could be an impressive new startup, a helpful software program, a little-known niche magazine or some other intriguing product. Whatever it is, now's your chance to make it known and help generate more interest in this invaluable tool.

Share a story about how it has helped you, or interview the owners/creators of the product and learn more about why they created it (especially if there are more well-known alternatives out there). It's a win-win: you get to spotlight a potential trend in the making, while the product you're showcasing gets more much-deserved attention.

Popular business author Guy Kawasaki does this regularly on his Holy Kaw! segment of alltop.com. For example, did you know there's a monastery of bonsai tree sculptors in Conyers, Georgia[6]? For anyone interested in bonsai cultivation, it's definitely something worth highlighting.

What's something that you feel doesn't get the kind of exposure it should?

6 Meet the Bonsai Monks of Georgia
http://holykaw.alltop.com/meet-the-bonsai-monks-of-georgia

What is Something You Wish Your Customers Knew About Your Business?

Go ahead – let it out. This is your chance to give your customers a behind-the-scenes look at what your work is really like. You can also twist this prompt a bit to reflect "X Things Your (Insert Profession Here) Won't Tell You."

These can include the somewhat clichéd "I Don't Have the Authority to Give You a Discount" or "Time is Money", but can also include more specific points such as the difference between fixing "this one small thing", and outright scope creep.

Some examples include:

- 10 Things Your Babysitter Won't Tell You
  http://glo.msn.com/relationships/10-things-your-babysitter-wont-tell-you-4794.gallery

- 13 Things Your Pilot Won't Tell You
  http://www.rd.com/slideshows/13-things-your-pilot-wont-tell-you/

Look carefully at your most common customer issues and questions – do you notice a common thread? If so, take the time to write a post that elaborates on what you can and cannot do in your line of work.

What Unique Value(s) Do You Bring to Your Industry (And Your Blog) Every Day?

This prompt answers one of the core questions needed to develop a loyal audience of readers: why should I pay attention to you? What do you offer that no one else does?

If you don't know, ask a colleague, a friend or even your favorite clients. The answers may surprise you! This prompt is similar to a company's USP or Unique Selling Proposition. It's not just about what makes you different, but about why customers should do business with you – and not with your competition.

Remember: people buy solutions to a problem – they aren't buying your product or service or even your expertise, but how that expertise translates into a solution for them. Write a post that accentuates your unique talents and strengths, and then translate those into something that matters to your audience.

If you're still struggling, why not ask your clients why they ultimately chose you? Your customers can often provide the best value statement there is.

Why Do You Love What You Do?

It sounds like such a simple question, but you can really put forth some deep answers to this one. It could be a single moment that changed you, a spark that reignited your desire for change, or something you fell into by way of a happy accident. But few things rev up discussion like sharing your passion for your particular blog topic.

This isn't to say that you should love what you do every day, and couldn't imagine doing anything else. Every job has its ups and downs. But writing about your interest in your topic and why you've stayed committed to it all this time will likely inspire others to follow in your footsteps, while carving out their own path.

It's also perfectly okay if you didn't start out loving your topic, but gradually grew into it over time. It's also normal to note that your happiness and excitement for your topic came out of the thrill of an accomplishment or success, rather than a lifelong passion for something.

In any case – write about it! Enthusiasm is contagious!

What Does Your Company Name Mean to You?

This introspective-style prompt will get you thinking – and may even be the catalyst for some interesting stories, such as what's happened with Apple.

Answers on how the company got its name range from the simple (the founders would name the company Apple if they were unable to think of a better name by 5:00 that evening), to the innovative (the relationship of the apple to Sir Isaac Newton and how it spawned new concepts in science and how we view the world).

But the name itself evokes a lot more than that to its fans and followers. Today, the company is synonymous with technology that's sleek, desirable and professional.

While your own company story may not spring into a tech behemoth from such humble origins, sharing how and why you chose the name will certainly make for some interesting reading on your blog!

Fascinating Facts You Didn't Know About _____

This prompt doesn't just have to stick solely to your particular blog topic, but could also focus on an important person in your field.

For example, the *HowStuffWorks* blog shares a slideshow of "10 Cool Things You Didn't Know About Stephen Hawking", such as that he was once a part of his university rowing team, and that while in grade school, his grades were mediocre at best[7].

Posts like these are pure entertainment, and are sure to get a great deal of social media mentions based on the sheer curiosity factor alone. Who knows, you may even learn a few interesting tidbits about the history of your industry or its pioneers in the process!

[7]: 10 Cool Things You Didn't Know About Stephen Hawking
http://science.howstuffworks.com/dictionary/famous-scientists/physicists/10-cool-things-stephen-hawking.htm#page=0

Anatomy of a _____

Here's your opportunity to share some inside knowledge about your specialty, product or service. What makes your version unique or better? Break it down into individual pieces or sections, and explain each part.

Your anatomy post doesn't even have to highlight a tangible object. One example, "Anatomy of a Computer Virus" uses video motion graphics to highlight how Stuxnet, the sophisticated virus/weapon that infected Iran's nuclear facilities, was able to get access to and disable vital systems, using an array of intelligent methods and exploits[8].

What concept or product could you break down and simplify for your audience? You could even go a step further and turn the post into an infographic[9] – which greatly increases its reach and exposure, especially through social networks like Twitter, Facebook and Pinterest.

[8] Stuxnet – Anatomy of a Computer Virus:
http://www.youtube.com/watch?v=YWAZXYzZpNA

[9] An infographic is a way to present information and statistics visually using charts and images. You can create your own infographics by using drag-and-drop visual editors including **Easel.ly, Infogr.am** and **Piktochart.com**

What Your _____ Reveals About You

This is a fascinating prompt that's sure to get a lot of responses, since everyone is intrigued by mysterious insights into their lives or personalities.

Case in point – the Association for Dressings and Sauces (I promise I'm not making that up!) released a survey titled "What Your Favorite Condiment Reveals About You"[10].

Some results were to be expected (salsa lovers are motivated and have that hot-and-spicy "kick" about their personalities), and others were downright odd (mustard users rated themselves as more shy than members of other groups).

These types of posts are meant to pique your readers' curiosity, and they're certainly an entertaining read. Posts like this do exceptionally well on social networks, particularly when they're turned into a type of quiz or survey that lets the reader share their results on Facebook or other sites.

SnapApp[11] is one such quiz builder which allows you to create a fully brandable Facebook quiz. It's a great method of converting a blog post into something with the potential for a much larger reach.

[10] What Your Favorite Condiment Reveals About You
http://www.dressings-sauces.org/pressroom_revealsaboutyou.html

[11] SnapApp Facebook Quizzes
http://www.snapapp.com/capabilities/facebook-quizzes

Why I Don't Use _____

If you're one of the last holdouts to join a particular service or use a particular product, this is the perfect time to let your blog audience know why. It may be for personal reasons, professional reasons, or because you simply don't have time.

But as more and more readers come to your blog, they'll likely have questions about particular products or services in your niche, and why you don't use them. It's better to answer it all in one blog post rather than keep fending off questions!

Some examples include:

Otterbox CEO: Why I don't use Social Media:
http://www.inc.com/curt-richardson/otterbox-ceo-why-i-dont-use-social-media.html

Mother Nature Network: Why I don't wear sunscreen:
http://www.mnn.com/health/fitness-well-being/blogs/why-i-dont-wear-sunscreen

Remember that some of your readers may disagree with your choice and (vehemently) persuade you to change your mind – moderate your comments well and be on the lookout for people who are just trying to stir up disagreements rather than add to the conversation.

How Would You Change _____?

This prompt is meant to guide you in sharing your thoughts on how you'd change some important mainstay of your niche. It could be a product, a service, a common process or some other well-known application that seems to be "set in stone".

The focus of what you'd change can be as deep and wide-ranging as something like healthcare, or something as simple and straightforward as a movie ending. Whatever it is, list the ways that you feel it could be improved on and invite your audience to give their own insights.

Some examples include:

How would you change foster care?
http://adoption.about.com/u/ua/fostering/if_i_could_change_the _foster_care_system.01.htm

Mini Goodwood – How Would You Change It?
http://www.motoringfile.com/2013/01/01/mini-goodwood-how-would-you-change-it/

Share how you'd change something and then invite your readers to contribute their own ideas. Invite them to speak from personal experience if they feel comfortable, and who knows, maybe your post will be the drop that ripples across your entire industry!

Ask The _____

Here's your opportunity to build your authority and gain more credibility for your blog. Entire websites (some making as much as six figures a year or more) have been built around this one concept entirely, so you may want to make it a regular feature of your blog!

Tim Carter of AskTheBuilder.com started his website in 1995 and it looks much the same now as it did even back then (when websites were far less sophisticated!).

Not only does Tim invite users to ask questions, but he also records and shares his answers on YouTube – tapping into an audience outside his blog to expand his reach considerably. He also makes extra money through his site by having sponsors and by promoting his favorite tools via Amazon.com's affiliate program.

Another example, AskTheHeadhunter.com (also online since 1995), has gained news attention from PBS, Dow Jones, and numerous other media outlets. In addition to their Q & A section, they also regularly invite guest speakers, expose job hunting scams, and feature a wide range of resources.

Look for ways to turn your blog communication into more than just a one-way street!

Chapter 3: Working Together with Other Bloggers

Nobody ever said you had to do everything yourself – and you shouldn't! Blogs can be collaborative, and help you reach new readers and subscribers in ways you could never do alone.

U.K. blogger Sarah Arrow's site, Birds on the Blog[1], became a collaborative effort between a group of ladies who decided that "women blogging" didn't necessarily have to revolve around changing diapers or which lipstick color to try.

Since then, Birds on the Blog has ranked in the Forbes Top 100 Blogs for Women for three years. While it generally focuses on the broad topic of women in business, it also has a lighter-hearted side, with posts such as "How to Use Your Breakfast Cereal as a Relationship Counsellor"[2].

Maybe scoring an interview with the top blogger in your niche is still a dream that's a little far out of reach right now. Even if they won't give you the time of day, there's still a very good chance that you can reach out to like-minded individuals and work together on coming up with great post ideas, contributing to an in-depth series that looks at a particular issue, or just giving each other feedback.

This section highlights a wide range of posts that you can tackle together with others in a way that benefits everyone!

---

[1] Birds on the Blog
http://www.birdsontheblog.co.uk

[2] **http://www.birdsontheblog.co.uk/how-to-use-your-breakfast-cereal-as-a-relationship-counsellor/**

Conduct an Interview with a Fellow Blogger Whose Point of View on a Topic is Completely Different than Yours

It's good to have a refreshingly different point of view on your blog every now and then – even (and perhaps especially!) if they're a competitor of yours. Invite them to share their view on a topic of interest to your audience and why they feel so strongly about it, and ask if you can do the same on their blog.

This "post swap" of sorts might sound as if you're opening the castle gates and letting the "enemy" waltz right in – but no one ever said that the other blogger has to be a direct competitor. In fact, if you offer products or services within the same niche, you'll both benefit by interviewing each other and gaining different perspectives on the matter.

Some blogs even use this prompt as a pivotal part of their business. Blogger Nicole Dean uses this method on her blog[3] in the form of "Expert Briefs". She sends out a question to fellow bloggers she likes and respects, and then compiles their answers into one large post along with her own point of view and conclusion.

Because she includes a disclaimer that gives her broader rights on what to do with the content beyond the post itself, she has been able to turn much of the content from these briefs into a book which is now sold on Amazon.com.

[3] Why Publish Collaborative Blog Posts?
http://thefutureofink.com/become-famous-like-oprah-publish-collaborative-blog-posts/

Leverage the Momentum of Conferences

Here's a fantastic idea I picked up from Luis Fernandes and Social Marketing Today[4]. Look at the agenda of upcoming conferences in your niche. These should already spark some ideas for your writing – but don't stop there.

Most big conferences have a Twitter hashtag[5] associated with them. People at the conference will be tweeting what's happening live, so schedule your blog post around the time that the topic is expected to be front and center at the conference and in the Twitterverse.

Not only will you pick up visitors and traffic from Twitter, but you'll also be catching the attention of people who are tweeting at the conference, as well as their followers and others who are following that particular hashtag.

[4] Luis Fernandes – Profile:
http://openviewpartners.com/people/luis-fernandes/

[5] What is a Hashtag?
http://en.wiktionary.org/wiki/hashtag

Create a Blog Pack to Expand Your Reach and Improve Your Accountability

This prompt is based off of an idea originally posted several years ago by Michael Martine of Remarkablogger[6]. A blog pack consists of a group of individuals who agree to comment on each other's posts, give constructive feedback, and share them across various social networks for added exposure.

Blog posts work best when all of the people in the group are relatively equal in terms of website traffic, online popularity and expertise level. This way, you can all work together to improve your sites and generate more exposure more effectively than working alone.

As Michael notes in his original post – do this with other up-and-coming bloggers you like and respect – not as a way to exploit people for your own gain. If you have any misgivings about members of the group, all your efforts will feel fake and forced – and your followers and subscribers will see right through it.
Still, when done positively with shared goals and mutual accountability in mind, you can all achieve more with less effort.

[6] Michael Martine – Create a Blog Pack to Get Blog Traffic and Subscriptions
http://remarkablogger.com/2008/05/14/create-a-blog-pack-to-get-blog-traffic-and-increase-subscriptions/

What Are Some Best Practices from a Corporation Outside of Your Own Niche?

When it comes to highlighting innovation and best practices, it pays to look outside of your own industry and see what other companies are doing. Think people wouldn't want to rent out a room in your apartment when you're halfway across the country at a conference? The idea was crazy enough to fly – and in 2012, earned AirBNB[7] a spot on Fast Company's 50 Most Innovative Companies.

Now, simply highlighting these companies' creative strategies is a good start – but how can you apply them to your own business or industry?

Wild Apricot[8] took a look at the Fast Companies article and discovered four things that membership organizations could learn from them – ranging from Apple's "Walk the Talk" to Southern New Hampshire University's "Relentlessly Reinvent" – all things that any organization conscious of dwindling numbers could recognize and react on.

Consult with other bloggers in your topic and have a brainstorming session. What are some unique, innovative, game-changing strategies that other startups are doing to make themselves stand out? How can you apply these methods to your own blog?

[7] Fast Company – AirBNB Most Innovative Companies
http://www.fastcompany.com/3017358/most-innovative-companies-2012/19airbnb

[8] Wild Apricot – 4 Things Membership Organizations Can Learn from Innovative Companies
http://www.wildapricot.com/blogs/newsblog/2013/01/07/4-things-membership-organizations-can-learn-from-innovative-companies

X (Topic) Mistakes that Even the Pros Make

Let's face it – nobody's perfect. And when you discover some of the bone-headed mistakes that even experts make, your readers won't feel so bad about their flub-ups either. You can go several different directions with this post – asking your readers to submit their own face-palm moments, interviewing other professionals in your industry, or even posting cringe-worthy mistakes of your own.

This type of post isn't meant to discourage or lambaste others, but to show that we're all human, and to turn what could have been a serious error into something we can all look back at and say, "Hey, I've done that too!"

Well-known blogs periodically highlight their own rookie mistakes, such as Search Engine Watch's "3 Big PPC Mistakes Even Pros Make"[9] or The Motley Fool's "7 Rookie Mistakes Even the Pros Make"[10].

You can also add to this prompt by demonstrating what to do instead, so that others don't encounter the same pitfalls you or your readers did when they first started out. Better yet, turn these lessons into an infographic that can have greater reach across social networks!

[9] Search Engine Watch – 3 Big PPC Mistakes Even Pros Make
http://searchenginewatch.com/article/2241384/3-Big-PPC-Mistakes-Even-Pros-Make-How-to-Avoid-Them

[10] The Motley Fool – 7 Rookie Mistakes Even the Pros Make
http://www.fool.com/investing/general/2012/01/31/7-rookie-mistakes-even-the-pros-make.aspx

Winning Habits of Extraordinary People

We all want to know what the "secret sauce" is that makes great people great. While you may not be able to reach the upper echelons of celebrity bloggers in your topic, you can ask the up-and-coming bloggers you look to as role models or even "sidekicks" on your writing journey – what are some habits that changed your life?

You can even step out on the social path and ask your Facebook friends, Twitter followers or Pinterest pals about the habits that make their lives better. The good news is, this kind of inspirational topic works for nearly any blog, and is always a reminder of the things we should strive to make a part of our own daily habits.

What's more, it doesn't just have to be general life habits. You can focus on the feel-good theme, like Parents Magazine did when they profiled "17 Habits of Very Happy Moms"[11] or you can focus on a more central topic like productivity habits, eating habits, or even sleep habits, such as Entrepreneur Magazine's "7 Sleep Habits of Successful Entrepreneurs"[12].

Invite your readers to share their own successful habits and you'll be well on your way to enjoying a cascade of comments of others chipping in and offering their own advice or thanking you for sharing yours!

[11] Parents Magazine – 17 Habits of Very Happy Moms
http://www.parents.com/parenting/moms/healthy-mom/17-habits-of-very-happy-moms/

[12] Entrepreneur Magazine – The 7 Sleep Habits of Successful Entrepreneurs
http://www.entrepreneur.com/article/228166

How Did You First Get into Your Chosen Subject?

This introspective blog prompt is designed to get you to reminisce about how and why you first started getting into the topic you're blogging about. Whether you're working toward replacing your full-time income, or you've turned your blog into a profitable hobby or community – telling your story is immensely cathartic, not to mention inspirational for others.

Maybe you finally hit on an area where you could take steps to reach a goal you've always dreamed of, like Andrew Castro's "Why I Started My Own Clothing Line"[13], or Inc.'s interview with unusual business founders on why they started their own businesses[14].

Ask your fellow bloggers and readers to share their own stories – some will amaze, delight, or even infuriate you. From the unknown entrepreneur who realized her true passion after being fired for having Lyme Disease, to honouring a loved one, our reasons for blogging and building a business are as varied and unique as our own fingerprints.

What's yours?

[13] Andrew Castro – Medium.com – Why I Started My Own Clothing Line
https://medium.com/what-i-learned-building/d915a41bef5

[14] Inc.com – Why I Started a Business – 5 Unusual Founder Stories
http://www.inc.com/john-brandon/5-real-founder-stories-what-really-motivated-you.html

What Would You Be Doing Right Now if You Weren't in Your Current Industry?

It may seem counter-intuitive to go back and relive the past, but somewhere along the way, there was a turning point where you chose the current path you're on.

But if you hadn't, what would you be doing instead?

You don't have to tackle this subject as a black-and-white setup of "If I weren't blogging, I'd be slogging my way through [insert less-than-stellar choice here], but rather think about some of the life choices you made (or the choices life made for you) that got you to this point.

Your readers and other bloggers likely have similar stories they'd love to share, so open up those comments and start a discussion on the setbacks, swerves and other events that got you here.

Some people even found their current niche when they stopped reading other blogs about it, or even when they could no longer do the thing they loved most (if even temporarily), like Hungry Runner Girl[15].

---

[15] Hungry Runner Girl – How I Started Hungry Runner Girl
http://www.hungryrunnergirl.com/2013/01/how-i-started-the-hungry-runner-girl-and-tips-to-start-your-own-blog.html

Write about an Opportunity You Missed or a Chance You Didn't Take – And How You Would Do Things Differently Today

Everyone has regrets. Sometimes, we look back at missed opportunities and wring our hands that such a chance will never happen again – when so many other opportunities are passing us by while we're busy lamenting over what's passed.

This post is designed to inspire and motivate your readers to not let the same thing happen to them, and is best when done with a group of fellow bloggers. This way, you get multiple points of view and perspectives that show the many paths one's life (whether blogging or otherwise) can take – and how you all ended up here.

Even Sir Richard Branson of Virgin has wondered about what could've been[16]. So you're certainly not alone!

On that note, "doing things differently" doesn't have to mean that those things are wrong and you're convinced you're on the right track. But missing opportunities forces us to be introspective and ask "why?" and hopefully take steps to make changes so that next time, we'll be ready to pounce.

This prompt can reflect an opportunity that slipped in your blogging arena, or an area of your life that, looking back, you wish you could've improved.

Either way, it will serve to remind others that we all only have a finite amount of time on this rock, and we'd best not only open the door when opportunity knocks, but invite it to stay for dinner.

[16] Opportunity Missed
http://www.virgin.com/richard-branson/opportunity-missed

Write About Something You Wish Someone Would Invent (Or Improve Upon, if it Has Already Been Invented)

Invite your fellow bloggers to contribute to this list and you're sure to get some unusual, innovative and "oh yeah! We could really use that!" responses.

Whether it's less electronic gadget overload (do we really need a mobile phone *and* a handheld gaming device *and* a music player?) or an outright challenge to the de-facto standard of doing things in your topic area, you'll be surprised at some of the interesting responses you're sure to get when you ask this question to other bloggers.

And if you think your invention idea can't go anywhere – consider this:

A dissatisfaction with the then-current style of American track running shoes led a guy and his coach to experiment with pouring and shaping rubber in a waffle iron to increase traction on the soles of their shoes. They later founded a company called Nike. [17]

And speaking of running, even Runners World magazine has some creative product ideas featured in a slideshow on their blog. These range from common-sense ideas from the ClimaBubble (15 degrees outside? You can still go for a run!) to the so-strange-it-just-might-work Road ID Candy Bracelet for emergencies and a quick sugar boost.

Even if the thing has already been invented, there are surely ways to improve on it. Not every invention solves a problem as accurately or efficiently as it could. Invite your readers to share their own ideas and, if nothing else, have a bit of fun imagining what could be!

[17] Inventor of the Week: Archive
http://web.mit.edu/invent/iow/bowermanknight.html

[18] Running Inventions We'd Like to See
http://www.runnersworld.com/photos/running-inventions-wed-like-to-see

What is the Greatest Recent Invention in Your Line of Work? How has it Improved What You Do?

Another prompt about inventions – but this one takes a closer look at the real game-changers in your industry. Notice I said *recent* invention, so all you bloggers out there can't rave about the printing press or the computer.

Case in point – you might not think much of composting, but if you work in the green industry, city-wide curbside composting is a big deal, helping to keep as much as 34% of trash (mostly yard trimmings and discarded food) out of landfills and back into gardens [19].

This type of community movement can in turn affect the overall cleanliness of the city, turn vacant lots into gardens, and cut back on methane emissions – all potential blog topics in their own right.

And that's not even considering any other green inventions, such as light bulbs, bike rental kiosks and even "green burials"[20].

Invite other bloggers to share the invention that has most impacted their work and how, and watch the discussion grow roots of its own and take off!

[19] Why Doesn't Your City Have Curbside Composting?
http://www.motherjones.com/environment/2012/09/why-doesnt-your-city-have-curbside-composting

[20] Green Funerals: How to Make an Eco-Exit
http://www.huffingtonpost.com/2008/04/22/green-funerals-how-to-mak_n_97940.html

What Are Some Resources that are Well Worth the Money You Spent on Them? Which Resources Aren't?

We all have purchases in our topic area that we can look back and say we got our money's worth out of them. And then there are...the others.

Things that are worth/not worth it can range from a product or a service, to degrees [21], and even people [22].

Be prepared to defend your choice, particularly if it's part of an ongoing (and sometimes heated) debate – think PC gaming vs. console or Mac vs. Windows.

Ask your fellow bloggers to chip in with their own recommendations and share what they wish they hadn't purchased. These are typically bigger investments but can also be software programs, specific tools, or even infomercial gadgets.

Chances are, both options will go a long way toward informing your readers on what choices to make (or avoid) as they continue to learn about the topic you're sharing.

[21] B-School Remorse: When the Degree is Just Not Worth It
http://management.fortune.cnn.com/2013/11/08/mba-remorse-business-school/

[22] Tony Romo is Not Only Worth the Money, He's Underpaid.
http://www.forbes.com/sites/tomvanriper/2013/10/07/tony-romo-is-not-only-worth-the-money-hes-underpaid/

What is Something that Annoys You about the Business You're In? How Would You Change It?

Blogs are perfect for airing annoyances. From the little things to major issues, it can do your soul good to get it off your chest. Chances are, your fellow bloggers can commiserate with you and share their own pet peeves.

But where things really get interesting (and to prevent this post from turning into a complaint-fest), is the *how would you change it* part. Sure, it feels cathartic to vent, but your readers would get little value from a full-scale rant.

By sharing how you'd change it, you give your readers a sense of not only what not to do in your line of work, but also possibly become the spark for making the changes you're hoping for. Fellow bloggers may be able to share how they overcame those annoyances or give you ideas or tools they used in the process.

One forum, the Garage Journal, includes a thread where members share what annoys them most about the fabrication industry [23]. Even if you know nothing about fabrication, some of the photos and stories will make you cringe.

[23] The Things that Annoy You in the Fabrication Industry?
http://www.garagejournal.com/forum/showthread.php?p=3070350

What's Something You Learned About Your Topic that You Wish Someone Had Told You About Ahead of Time?

Whether you're blogging as a way to make extra money or just to share your thoughts, there are always going to be things that you wish you'd gotten advice about before you jumped in.

For example, a graduate at Rasmussen College who became a graphic designer wished she would've been told that yes, you still have to use math and that it's about more than learning graphic design software[24].

You don't even have to tackle a particular career field, as one blogger noted when she was first diagnosed with ovarian cancer. For patients undergoing chemotherapy (and the family and friends who support them), knowing what to expect from someone who's been there can make the process seem a lot less overwhelming[25].

Throughout all your experiences, think about the things you wish you would've known beforehand. Turn this post into a collaborative effort with other bloggers and you'll have a sizeable chunk of real-life advice that your readers can really learn from and appreciate.

[24] What I Wish Someone Had Told Me Before Becoming a Graphic Designer
http://www.rasmussen.edu/degrees/design/blog/wish-someone-told-me-before-becoming-graphic-designer/

[25] Ten Things I Wish My Doctor Told Me About Chemotherapy
http://hubpages.com/hub/Ten-Things-I-Wish-My-Doctor-Told-Me-About-Chemotherapy

Write about Something that Raised Your Expectations, but the Result Was Nothing Like You Expected

We all hold high hopes that everything is going to finally turn out fine if we just do or buy that one thing. Commercials even play on this hopefulness by showing happy families, cute babies, fast cars and everyday people surrounded by gorgeous models.

We'd all like to think that somehow, maybe we could enjoy a slice of that paradise too.

This prompt springboards off of that expectation – and the result can be either good or bad. Maybe you found an unexpected and better use for something you bought, or the product or service fell flat on its face and then threw itself down a flight of stairs for good measure.

You could even take this prompt and apply it to an event, conference or hot topic in your industry. For example, the healthcare sector is currently infatuated with the idea of big data[26] but some issues still exist.

By writing about a product, service or issue that similarly affects you or the topic of your blog, you'll not only give your readers more insights into something that they, too, may have been following or considered attending – but were also looking for opinions first.

If you're writing about a product that's highly popular or in-demand, be prepared to recognize people coming to "its" aid, or recommending alternatives in an attempt to funnel your traffic to their affiliate links. Health and weight loss supplements in particular seem to be vulnerable to this type of hijacking.

---

[26] High Expectations for Big Data Among Healthcare Execs, But Hurdles Remain **http://www.fiercehealthit.com/story/high-expectations-big-data-among-healthcare-execs-hurdles-remain/2013-12-06**

Dealing with Something Unpleasant, but Unavoidable

This prompt lets you share how you overcome the little-known but all-too-familiar aggravations you face in your particular topic. From using an organic solution on weeds[27] to coming face to face with an adult bully at work or in your neighborhood[28], dealing with "stuff" is one of those things that everyone can relate to.

By sharing your strategies, tips and techniques, you'll be able to give your readers the next best thing to one-on-one help (or at the very least, someone to commiserate with!)

Don't forget to let people know what may happen if they continue to ignore the problem, as well as how to prevent it from happening again, if possible.

If the "something unpleasant" relates to a person – like a co-worker or boss, let readers know how to take the next logical step if just "dealing" doesn't do the trick. Remember, people are looking to you as an authority and an advisor. Know where your role ends and their responsibilities begin.

[27] How to Deal with Weeds in Your Garden the Organic Way
http://www.organicgardening.com/learn-and-grow/weeds-organic-strategy

[28] How to Deal with Adult Bullies
http://www.everydayhealth.com/emotional-health/how-deal-with-adult-bullies.aspx

Describe a Good Experience with a Product or Service You Bought Online

You took the plunge. You ordered online and were more than satisfied with the results. The company went above and beyond to keep you updated on the progress of your order, followed up to see if you had any questions, and gave you lots of helpful advice to get started.

Sounds like the kind of site you can't help but brag about, right?

So why keep your experience to yourself? Share your story with your readers, and what the company did to go above and beyond your expectations. Your post could even start off on a sour note – with a competitor stepping in to save the day.

Author Pamela Slim shared a blog post several years ago[29] about retailers who don't pressure you into buying, but rather entice you through their spectacular customer service. One of the companies she mentioned was Peet's Coffee, who went out of their way to send her some coffee as a Christmas gift for her continued kind notes about their service on Twitter and Facebook.

What are some companies that have astounded you with their quality products, outstanding service or overall "with-it-ness" in business? Put them in the spotlight on your blog and invite fellow bloggers in your industry to share their experiences too!

[29] Extrasensory Customer Experience
http://www.escapefromcubiclenation.com/2006/09/07/extrasensory-customer-experience/

Who are Some People in Your Industry that You'd Like to Meet, and Why?

We all have industry role models. These are the people we look up to, either through what they've done with their blog, or what they've been able to do because of it. One example for entrepreneurs is Seth Godin[30], now an author, speaker and mentor to many marketers and online business owners.

Aside from his books, Godin is perhaps most famous for Squidoo, a community-based network that allows individuals to create "lenses" (pages) on topics of interest. These lenses can contain text, images, and even links to affiliate products such as books or movies from Amazon.com.

Fifty percent of the revenues generated through these pages are given to the owners (called lensmasters) and 5% is donated to charity. In November of 2013, the Squidoo Charity Fund was able to donate $60,000 to causes including Acumen Fund, Room to Read and Save the Children.

Who's a rainmaker in your industry, and why would you like to meet them? Invite your fellow bloggers to create their own shortlists on your blog and link back to the sites of your mentors. Who knows, the attention might just net their interest and help you reach your goal!

[30] Seth Godin
http://en.wikipedia.org/wiki/Seth_Godin

What are Some of the Best Things You've Done so Far this Year?

This blog prompt can shape up to be a meaningful accomplishment list when done together with other bloggers. It's not meant to brag-- but rather inspire. Oftentimes, the plans and resolutions we make end up taking a completely different turn, as what happened for one mom blogger in an online issue of Parenting Today[31].

In this case, one simple phone call ended up having a life-changing impact on her daughter and the family as a whole.

There are people out there right now struggling with the very same things that challenged you. Share your stories – the ups as well as the downs, and detail how you overcame them. If you haven't quite been triumphant, that's okay too – be real about the struggles that came as a part of the "best thing" you've done.

This type of post can not only reach out to help others remember that sometimes the simplest things can have the biggest impact, but also serves as a guidepost for you to look back and consider how far you've come. Pat yourself on the back!

[31] The Best Thing I Did For My Family in 2012
http://www.todaysparent.com/blogs/tracys-mama-memoirs/the-best-thing-i-did-for-my-family-in-2012/

Is the Customer Always Right? Is Honesty Always the Best Policy? Take a Cliché and Prove it Right

So far in your life, you've had experiences that show just how clichéd clichés can be. But sometimes, your attitude really can determine your altitude. Take a popular cliché and prove it right, citing experiences you've had that worked out better because of this common advice.

Be forewarned that there will be commenters who will debate you on this – citing from their own experiences. And of course, we've all had scenarios where the customer wasn't always right or something really did feel like it was going to kill you instead of make you stronger. Acknowledge that these clichés aren't right all the time – but focus on when they are.

Remember, inside all of these overused sayings is a kernel of powerful truth that applies to everyday life – sharing it with your readers, along with a story, real-life experience, or professional insight, can show us all that there's a reason these timeless words of wisdom endure.

Having trouble coming up with a good cliché? What about:

- The Grass is Always Greener on the Other Side – Is the chase part of the fun of trying to get what someone else has?

- You Can't Please Everyone – No matter what you do in life, there will always be people trying to bring you down. Often, your success is what challenges their insecurities.

- Ignorance is Bliss – Were things really simpler when you were a child? What did you consider happiness to be then versus now?

- Better Safe than Sorry – Was there ever a time when you were sorry that you played it safe? Or were you glad you didn't take that risk in the end?

What to Ask Your _____

When working with someone in your niche or industry for the first time, it's likely that your customer has a lot of questions. Whether you're in the remodelling business or you run a day care, there are bound to be questions that you'd hope your clients would ask – so why not share them?

This prompt has the potential to open up a lot of discussion between you, your fellow bloggers and your audience on crucial questions that, if asked, can help you avoid misunderstandings and miscommunications.

The Harvard Business Review, for instance, goes into great detail on what to ask your "Numbers People"[32] – the people that crunch and analyse numbers that lead to data-driven decisions. It has to do with gathering and analysing data correctly – potentially a conversation that a CEO would have with their financial manager, but the same prompt can apply for nearly any type of business, from electricians to veterinarians.

So what questions should people ask someone in your line of work? Ask your readers and fellow bloggers to contribute as well and you'll end up with a well-stocked list that no consumer should be without.

[32] What to Ask Your "Numbers People"
http://blogs.hbr.org/2013/07/what-to-ask-your-numbers-people/

The 10 Commandments of _____

Religion aside, your business, organization or hobby likely has a few set rules that everyone should obey in order to get the best possible results or outcome. Here's your chance to list them so that newcomers can "learn the ropes", and veterans can get a refresher.

Case in point – Search Engine Journal, a highly respected website on optimizing one's website for search engines (among other things), posted the 10 Commandments of a Great Guest Posting[33].

With common sense commandments that range from "Thou Shalt Not Write Drivel" to "Thou Shalt Reciprocate", these types of posts serve as a good reminder to help people get back on track and fully understand what to do, and not to do, in order to learn a bit more about your profession or hobby.

In the case of guest blogging, there was a period of time where everyone was a self-proclaimed guest blogger, which lead to a lot of half-baked articles on well-known blogs – simply because they'd forgotten (or never learned) the original guidance and advice that makes a guest post great.

What are ten things you could remind your readers of so that they're steered in the right direction?

[33] The 10 Commandments of a Great Guest Posting
http://www.searchenginejournal.com/10-commandments-great-guest-posting/80845/

The Golden Rules of _____

Similar to the Ten Commandments, the Golden Rule(s) of _____ share those unbreakable (and often unspoken) rules of your topic. For beginners, having this set of pristine guidelines gives them a lofty goal to aim for and helps to prevent missteps along the way.

If your particular subject doesn't have its own set of Golden Rules, why not tackle this post with a more esoteric bent, such as what Service Untitled did with their Golden Rules of Customer Loyalty[34].

Some of the points mentioned in their article *should* be common sense, but you may not be surprised at how often they're forgotten. Things like appreciating your customer and valuing their feedback should be cornerstones of every company's customer service philosophy.

Other Golden Rules are more technical in nature, like setting up loyalty or reward programs, or creating a process to thank customers regularly. What are some Golden Rules for the work or industry you're in? What can your fellow bloggers add about their own topic?

[34] The Golden Rules of Customer Loyalty
http://www.serviceuntitled.com/the-golden-rules-of-customer-loyalty/2013/12/17/

How Do You Know When You've _____?

How do you know when you've "made it"? How do you know when you've gone too far? We all instinctively look for sign posts along the way that guide us when we've hit an all-important milestone or perhaps taken things a bit beyond their normal conclusion.

This prompt invites you to think about your own industry successes (or pitfalls), or even tackle something a bit more near and dear to you. Once that's done, reach out to other bloggers and ask them to share their own guide posts as well.

For example, one marketing blog asks "How Do You Know When You've Created a Successful Community[35]?" For many websites, their communities are the lifeblood of their business. But is there a point at which you can say "Yes, this is a resounding success"?

Remember that different people have vastly different measurements of success, failure or whatever their end goal might be. Respect the differences as much as the similarities and you'll create a lively environment that's ripe for discussion and the sharing of perspectives.

[35] How Do You Know When You've Created a Successful Community? http://www.damniwish.com/how-you-know-when-youve-created-a-successful-community/

Lessons Learned From _____

Sometimes, it takes an incredible experience gone awkwardly wrong (or haphazardly right) to teach you some important lessons. What would you do if you discovered that your latest post was the trending topic on Twitter or Facebook?

Etienne Garbugli created and uploaded a simple slideshow on time management before getting ready for a long weekend. He never could've predicted what happened next: his slideshow went viral.

It got picked up as a featured presentation on SlideShare, tweeted from LinkedIn, featured on BusinessInsider and a host of other well-known sites.

Millions of visitors saw his presentation. For any website owner, millions of views is a momentous occasion. But there were also some not-so-great moments. Etienne details them all on his personal blog[36]

What about you? What are some lessons you've learned from an experience that changed your life or impacted you in some way? Invite other bloggers to share their own experiences on their blogs and create a network of links that can provide mountains of insight in an afternoon.

[36] Going Massively Viral on SlideShare: Lessons Learned
http://www.etiennegarbugli.com/going-massively-viral-on-slideshare-lessons-learned/

Chapter 4: The Simple Things

Sometimes the simplest things can ignite a ripple-effect of comments and discussions on your blog. In the hustle and bustle of daily life, we all too often forget to stop and acknowledge the little things we can do to make a change or improvement.

This chapter will help you remind your readers, and yourself, of the little things that save time, help you feel or look better, or make you more productive!

If you need a little inspiration, consider these quick posts for when you don't have much time to write, but need to knock out a post quickly to stay on your blogging schedule (more about that in the final chapter!)

Go ahead – grab a prompt and start writing!

What (Users) Want

One of the simplest truths in blogging is to give your audience what they want. This all boils down to discovering the "common need" that all of the readers in your topic area have.

Maybe they want to take better care of their health, but they're always busy and have no time to cook better meals. Why not give them simple 4 and 5 ingredient "tried-and-true" recipes that they can throw in the crockpot?

This can also be reworked as "What I Want You to Know About (Topic) – and in this case, it can be a very raw and stark tell-all about an issue, condition or professional choice you're dealing with.

One example comes from Alysa of InspiredRD.com, a blogger, mom and celiac who exposes the hidden, and oftentimes scary truth about eating gluten-free[1]. Alysa is a dietician, which would seemingly make the transition to being "de-glutened" easier – but it hasn't.

In her post, "What I Want You to Know About Celiac Disease", she explains that even the small things, like handling pizza at her kids' birthday parties and needing to scrub her hands afterwards, or meeting friends for lunch and dreading what might be on the menu.

When doing your post, consider how these specific items fulfil a need, make an improvement, or expose the truth behind the issue – not just in your life, but in the lives of family, friends, colleagues, fellow bloggers, and your readers.

[1]What I Want You to Know About Celiac Disease
http://inspiredrd.com/2013/05/what-i-want-you-to-know-celiac-disease.html

What's a Good Way to Simplify or Organize Something Your Readers Might Find Difficult?

The new year is a great time for this blog prompt, but it's just as useful any other time of the year. Everyone has a moment where they're feeling overwhelmed and surrounded by clutter.

With this prompt, you don't have to tackle the big things (remember, we're keeping it simple in this chapter!), like organizing every facet of your life – but you can surely find areas where you've organized, simplified, explained or de-cluttered something that was seemingly too cumbersome for your readers.

Think of something you've managed to wrangle, either through your expertise or just by pure trial and error, and explain it to your users. You don't even have to write a post – you could create a simple how-to video, as Jill Duffy from PC Magazine did on How to Organize Your Spotify Playlist[2].

To do this, you can use a simple screen recording software like TechSmith's Camtasia: **http://www.techsmith.com/camtasia.html** - This screen sharing software lets you record mouse movements and items on your computer while you narrate over a microphone.

At $300, however, it's a bit pricey, so if you're on a tight budget, you might want to consider the open source screen recorder CamStudio: **http://camstudio.org/**. Although it doesn't have as many annotation and editing features as Camtasia, you can't beat free!

[2] Get Organized: How to Organize Your Spotify Playlist
http://www.pcmag.com/article2/0,2817,2427211,00.asp

The One Hour _____.

What could someone learn how to do in your topic of expertise that would only take them an hour at most? The internet is perfect for quick, easy-to-follow tutorials that even beginners can use. Everything from watercolours to brick ovens can be made (albeit crudely) in as little as sixty minutes.

The One Hour Bag[3] at AllFreeSewing is the perfect example of how something simple and elegant can be made with very little experience and few materials. As you're writing your own how-to, don't forget to define any terms or jargon your audience may be unfamiliar with, or where to buy specific tools that may be needed.

Oftentimes these simple "1 hour" how-to's can motivate people to finally take the first step they've been planning and learn how to create, organize or tackle a new technique or subject.

You can also expand these points later for intermediate or advanced readers who want to take what they've learned and go farther.

[3] The One Hour Bag
http://www.allfreesewing.com/Bags-and-Purses/One-Hour-Bag

Simple Things You Can Do To_____

This simple post is meant as a starting point to get even the most under-confident reader off the couch and moving toward their goal. Whether it's going green or staving off dementia, simple steps get people to take action.

One such example of this prompt at work comes from Forbes magazine. With all the media focusing on cell phone monitoring, computer hacking and device spying, Forbes came up with a simple yet decidedly important article on ten simple things you can do to protect your privacy[4].

From everyday common sense tips like password protecting your devices and paying cash for potentially embarrassing items, to more technology-involved steps like encrypting your hard drive and adding email authentication, following these steps makes it possible for anyone to secure all the devices and websites that are a part of their lives.

What steps can you give readers that are easy to do and can make a world of difference?

[4]10 Incredibly Simple Things You Can Do to Protect Your Privacy
http://www.forbes.com/pictures/fjff45jml/password-protect-your-devices-6/

Signs You're Secretly a(n) _____

You've always suspected there was something different about you –
maybe you get way too excited when there's a comic book
convention in town, or you have an unusual collection of old-timey
spy gadgets.

Whatever your secret indulgence, this blog post blows the lid off of
it, and gives tell-tale signs that other readers might also see a bit of
themselves in.

This post can also shine a spotlight on uncomfortable but honest pain
points that may very well save a life – such as signs of a secretly
abusive or manipulative relationship, or the secret signs of stress.

On the lighter-hearted side of things, people love quizzes or
revelations that confirm something they've always known about
themselves.

The Huffington Post posted an article back in August of 2013
showcasing secret signs of being an introvert[5] and as of this writing,
it has received over 183,000 shares on Facebook. Over 2,500
comments invite and provoke discussion from introverts and the
extroverts who love, but don't always understand them.

What are some "secret" signs that your readers are wondering about
themselves?

---

[5] 23 Signs You're Secretly an Introvert
**http://www.huffingtonpost.com/2013/08/20/introverts-signs-am-i-
introverted_n_3721431.html**

Why X is Beating Y

No, this isn't a payback for all those tough algebra questions in school – it's a prompt that's meant to shine some light on a finding that people never thought could've happened.

If you're involved in the technology sphere at all, you know how vocal and devoted Mac fans can be. In their minds, there is seemingly no competition between a Macbook and anything else.

They might be surprised to learn, then, that Chromebooks (by Google) beat out Macbooks in the coveted education sector[6].

This type of post has been applied to all kinds of businesses – Pepsi versus Coke, Costco versus Walmart, and Tesla versus Ford to name a few.

Could you look at two competing products in your industry – perhaps the reigning champion versus an up-and-coming underdog, or an old, name-brand versus a spirited start-up, and predict who will win?

These types of posts tend to generate heaps of discussion, both for and against the two contenders. Be prepared to moderate your blog comments to avoid any all-out "fan wars", but invite constructive debate and different perspectives that stay on topic!

With a headline like this – your readers will surely be asking themselves, "how is that even possible?!"

[6] Why Chromebooks Beat Macs
http://mashable.com/2013/12/30/why-chromebooks-beat-macs-in-commercial-sales-in-2013

Share Your Bookmarks

Depending on how long you've been blogging on your specific topic, you've likely built up quite an enviable list of bookmarks in your browser. Whether they're resources, how-tos, or ideas to chew on, chances are that your readers would find them equally interesting!

So if you're crunched for time, why not select a dozen of your favorites and share them?

As an example, well-known marketing blog Hubspot has shared ten free tools that every blogger should bookmark[7]. The list ranges from basic (Creative Commons, RSS readers) to advanced (searching data-rich websites) and everything in between.

What are some free or low-cost tools you could share with your own readership? What about a list of introductory tutorials for those new to your subject?

You could even invite your readers to do a bookmark-swap where they share a few of their resources in the comments. You may stumble across some real gems you didn't know about before!

[7] 10 Free Tools Every Blogger Should Bookmark
http://blog.hubspot.com/blog/tabid/6307/bid/33269/10-Free-Tools-Every-Business-Blogger-Should-Bookmark.aspx

How to Hack Your _____

This one needs a little bit of explanation. First, I don't advise you to show someone how to actually hack something. These days, thanks to sites like LifeHacker.com, hacking can also mean a way to boost productivity or uncover little-known secrets.

That's the kind of hacking that readers love!

These things typically require a bit more work to do than your typical reader is inclined to put in – but for those that do it, it usually means a substantial savings of money, effort, time, and so on.

Case in point – Independent Traveler shows readers how to hack their airfare[8], while the Bulletproof Executive shows busy businesspeople how to hack their sleep cycles for more restful sleep in less time[9].

And if you're thinking that this type of hacking is only for the adventurous or the workaholics among us – and your site just sells office chairs, well, you'll be glad to know that you can hack those too[10]!

What are some neat tweaks or techniques you've learned about your topic that could save your readers time, money, health and more?

[8] How to Hack Your Way to a Cheaper Airfare
http://www.independenttraveler.com/travel-tips/travelers-ed/how-to-hack-your-way-to-a-cheaper-airfare

[9] How to Hack Your Sleep
http://www.bulletproofexec.com/how-to-hack-your-sleep-the-art-and-science-of-sleeping/

[10] How to Hack Your Office Chair
http://www.wired.co.uk/magazine/archive/2013/10/how-to/hack-your-office-chair

The First Thing to Do When You _____ .

Whether it's your first job, your first baby or your first three weeks at college, knowing precisely what to do (and what not to do!) will save you a great deal of time, trouble and possibly even embarrassment!

Learning from someone who has been there and understands the uncertainty, frustration or fear can help many first-timers. Even if you're now the proud owner of a new gadget, say a new Android tablet[11], a few basic steps with screenshots illustrating the different areas can go a long way toward overcoming that technophobia and giving readers more comfort and confidence along the way.

Remember, everyone has been new at something. Help guide your readers when they're just starting out by getting them to take that all important step or two.

Give your readers some beginner advice on what you'd recommend they do if they're just starting out in your field of expertise. They'll love you for it!

[11] The First 6 Things You Need to Do With Your New Android Tablet
http://reviews.cnet.com/8301-3126_7-57615335/the-first-6-things-you-need-to-do-with-your-new-android-tablet/

Bloggers You Should Be Following

Just like with the bookmarks list on page 79, this prompt lets you feature a list of your favorite bloggers. Not only does it give you a chance to explain why you enjoy reading their blogs and following them on social media, but it also gives you the opportunity to spread out a bit of link love for the people you admire.

One example, from FitBie.com[12], shares 10 weight loss bloggers you should follow – and why. Their blogs not only give you inspiration and motivation when you're feeling stuck, but also show you just how far each of the bloggers has come from their own "stuck-ness", proving that anyone can create their own success story.

You can also turn these blog spotlights into a mini-slideshow via SlideShare.net and embed the code right on your site or share it via LinkedIn, Twitter or Facebook. Slideshare is free to use and it only takes a few minute to upload and create your own virtual slideshow – no technical experience necessary.

You can also take screenshots of the blog in question (see the helpful tools and resources in chapter 5 for software that helps you do this) or include photos of the bloggers themselves, so that you have a great introductory launch pad from right inside your own blog.

[12] 10 Weight Loss Bloggers You Should Follow
http://www.fitbie.com/slideshow/10-weight-loss-bloggers-you-should-follow

Write a Versus Post

When it comes to This vs. That, people can't help but secretly pick a favorite. Whether you're rooting for the underdog or a diehard fan of the reigning champion – take two (or three) things and have them virtually duke it out on your blog.

What are the pros and cons? Who ultimately reigns supreme – or is there even a real winner at all? Connect, the Digital Photography Review, did a versus post by pitting three competing items against each other: Smartphones, DSLR cameras and film.[13] They wondered, how far have we come since the days of film? How do today's SLRs compare to those from 10 years ago?

While it may seem like they're comparing apples to oranges (and the author even mentions this in their post), there was no universally "fair" way to test everything and really bring out the best of the photos, which is what readers really wanted to see.

It may very well turn out that there's no "winner" and that each item is better at different things – and that's fine too. If you do this type of comparison and want to be scientific about it, be sure to let readers know what steps you took in the comparison, the settings and other technical details.

And, although that extra step does take away from the simplicity of the post, you can almost certainly guarantee a good share of backlinks from fellow bloggers who are anxious to share your results with their own readers.

[13] Smartphones vs. DSLRs vs. Film
http://connect.dpreview.com/post/5533410947/smartphones-versus-dslr-versus-film

Checks to Ensure Your _____ is _____

Is your car ready for winter? Is your bike ready for the road? While a checklist may only seem like it's for vehicle maintenance, you can apply a few simple, straightforward reviews to almost any topic.

Whether it's making sure your network is secure[14] to property managers making sure their condominiums and homeowners' association are properly maintained[15], having the right set of checks and balances in place can save your readers a great deal of frustration and confusion.

What are some simple, stress-free checks you can advise your readers of to make sure they're in good shape when it comes to your topic area?

Remember, every step doesn't have to be in sequential order, but should be straightforward enough that someone can quickly go through the list to make sure they've got everything covered.

[14] 5 Checks You Must Run to Ensure Your Network is Secure
http://thehackernews.com/2013/01/5-checks-you-must-run-to-ensure-your.html

[15] Checks and Balances to Ensure a Healthy Condo and HOA
http://www.examiner.com/article/checks-and-balances-help-ensure-a-healthy-condo-and-hoa

Want To _____? Read This.

This prompt demands attention. It helps readers cut through the clutter and huge "tip lists" and gives them helpful, easy-to-follow advice that they can pick up and run with.

No matter what your readers want to do when they come to your blog for help or suggestions, this prompt gives them the low-down on what they should know before they begin.

Here are a few examples:

- Want Lilly Bulbs for Your Garden?
  http://bdlilies.blogspot.com/2011/12/want-lily-bulbs-in-your-garden-read.html

- Want to Be a Better Leader?
  http://www.inc.com/marc-barros/be-a-better-leader-in-2014.html

Another spin on this prompt is the common "So You've Decided to _____, Now What?"

Tid-bits of what you might consider to be "common sense" knowledge may never have occurred to beginners who want to learn more about your topic. The aforementioned leader piece above advises readers to "be vulnerable" – a word rarely associated with leadership, but very important when reaching out to others.

At first, your readers are going to take uncertain steps toward learning your particular subject of expertise. They might feel a lot like baby deer on a treadmill – but by presenting simple, easy to understand facts and an overview they can learn from, this prompt and the article that goes with it will help build up their confidence and stretch their comfort zone.

When _____ Goes Bad

What do you do when your best efforts backfire and tank? This prompt is all about salvaging what's left, or changing course and making corrections.

Case in point – Techcrunch recently shared what to do when growth hacking goes bad[16], while profiling some of the guiltiest companies and startups – usually apps or little-known social networks that spammed users and their friends with invitations.

Growth hacking is a term used to signify when a business focuses entirely on growing and spreading its brand in unconventional ways – think Twitter, Dropbox and many other Web 2.0 startups.

Used wisely, it can get a great number of people on board to try the service out. Done wrong, it can lead to a massive backlash of angry users.

So when something goes wrong in your blog's area of expertise – how do you deal with it?

 The point here is not exactly to name and shame others who have a less than stellar track record, but to advise people on the best path to take when their idea or strategy goes over like a lead balloon.

[16] When Growth Hacking Goes Bad
http://techcrunch.com/2014/01/03/when-growth-hacking-goes-bad/

What Happened When I Gave Up _____

This prompt doesn't have to involve major life changes – although it often does. Giving up smoking, eating junk and other bad habits are all great accomplishments – but what happens when you give up gluten from your diet[17] (assuming you are otherwise healthy), or when you give up email?[18]

Blog readers who are considering serious changes in their own lives – perhaps for their health, or perhaps just to try out disconnecting from the world for awhile, secretly want to know what to expect when they take the plunge.

Be the person who shares the story of how you gave up something you were sure you couldn't live without. How did it affect your daily life? Did the urge to go back get stronger or lesser as time went on?

Remember, giving up something that you feel like you depend on, or are even addicted to, is a bit of an experiment. Be serious about what you want to change and take measured steps to attain it – then let your blog readers know what happened along the way.

They'll appreciate the fact that you've travelled down this path and let them know what to look for – and what to avoid!

[17] I Gave Up Gluten and Here's What Happened
http://www.dailynews.com/health/20131112/i-gave-up-gluten-and-heres-what-happened

[18] What Happened When I Gave Up Email
https://www.openforum.com/articles/what-happened-when-i-gave-up-email/

Reasons Not To _____

This prompt is designed to go against common advice and do the exact opposite. For example, we're always told that when buying a house, it's important to pay off the mortgage before you retire. There's the notion of financial freedom, security and peace of mind.

But what if you didn't? An article in Forbes[19] gives seven reasons to consider not paying off your mortgage before you retire.

Of course, when your blog post goes against the grain of common advice, you can expect people to come out of the woodwork and tell you why you're wrong. That's understandable.

But this type of post also inspires more a more open mind and perhaps a change of perspective. If you don't follow the common advice or best practices, what could you do instead? Sometimes these kinds of posts need more creative answers – but I have complete confidence in you to come up with them ☺

[19] 7 Reasons Not to Pay Off Your Mortgage Before You Retire
http://www.forbes.com/sites/nancyanderson/2014/01/03/7-reasons-not-to-pay-off-your-mortgage-before-you-retire/

Show Off Your _____!

This is a great prompt that your readers can get involved with, using only their mobile phones or digital cameras. Put them in the spotlight and have them show off their best work using your blog as the platform.

Whether it's a garden design, a new website or even a wallet[20], a simple picture can do the talking for you, plus encourage other people to add their own comments and images.

The "Show Us Your Wallet" link below on Lifehacker, has over 100 comments with hundreds more waiting to be shared.
Who would've thought that something so small could be such a reflection of our personalities?

Alternatively, you could spin this prompt to reflect your own collection of tools or must-haves, such as one post on Digital Photography School did, entitled "What's In My Camera Bag". It's a helpful guide for anyone just starting out in the photography world.

What's something you could invite your readers to share images of on your blog? Let your readers show off their hard work or their first effort. Don't judge or critique – just share.

[20] Show Us Your Wallet
http://lifehacker.com/show-us-your-wallet-1495817724#replies

Why Most _____ Fail Within (Timeframe)

This post needs a bit of explaining – but once you understand the foundation behind it, you'll be able to tackle it with ease.

You see, most people never get to the point you're at. They think about starting a blog, or they start one and run out of steam after some time.

Or perhaps you've inspired them and they've started chipping away at learning whatever it is you're becoming an expert in – but they've hit a wall. They've given up.

Sadly, this is how even the best intentions end up. But why is that? Your task with this post is to look into what separates those that give up from those that ultimately overcome their challenge in your field.

Whether it's marketers failing in the era of big data[21] or why sugar addictions cause even the strongest diet willpower to crumble[22], exploring the reasoning behind the failures will help your readers understand the temptations and pitfalls that plague most of the people who try – and how they can be the rare, select few who beat the odds!

[21] Why Most Marketers Fail in the Era of Big Data
http://www.forbes.com/sites/gregsatell/2014/01/03/why-most-marketers-will-fail-in-the-era-of-big-data/

[22] Is Sugar Addiction Why So Many January Diets Fail?
http://www.npr.org/blogs/thesalt/2014/01/08/260781785/is-sugar-addiction-why-so-many-january-diets-fail

Gear That Won't Break the Bank

So maybe you want to run your first triathlon[23]… or you just want to make an amazing cup of espresso[24]. Whatever you're into, you want to do it right without spending a ton of money. That's where this prompt comes in.

As a blog author, you've been there, done that. You've tried a lot of products and learned through trial and error. So what products would you recommend to someone just starting out? Even something as simple and enjoyable as a cup of coffee can be turned into a work of art without much experience.

So go ahead – share your recommendations for your favorite inexpensive items for beginners who are looking to try out your subject of expertise for the first time. Don't forget to show pictures of the item in question (or a link to their website) if readers may be confused about which product to get.

This post is a great way to get long-time lurkers/first-time posters to join in on the conversation and start trying out your own hobby or interest in a way that's affordable and fun!

[23] Beginner's Triathlon Gear List
http://www.active.com/triathlon/articles/beginner-s-triathlon-gear-list-no-need-to-break-the-bank

[24] Coffee Gear that Won't Break the Bank
http://www.ineedcoffee.com/10/coffee-gear/

How to Handle it When...

Everyone faces obstacles or friction when they're attempting something brave. Whether it's asking for a raise or talking to your child about drug use, it's never an easy conversation.

In nearly every industry, there's always a couple of major points that stick with readers – perhaps they tried and tried to lose that extra 10 pounds, but the scale just won't budge. Or maybe, as profiled in Guy Kawasaki's AllTop.com (a personal favorite source of blog writing ideas!), no one recognizes your hard work[25].

What do you do? How do you cope?

Better yet, where is the line between your feelings or needs, and everyone else's? Some people just don't respond the way you'd expect. How should you deal with that?

Of course, no one can have all the answers, which makes this post a great reminder to open the digital podium and let your readers come forward to share their own stories. You may even discover an entirely new or novel way of dealing with something admittedly difficult.

[25] How to Handle It When No One Recognizes Your Hard Work
http://holykaw.alltop.com/how-to-handle-it-when-no-one-recognizes-your-hard-work

Lessons Learned from Losing $ in _____

Sometimes, what seems like a great investment at the time just doesn't pay off. Although this prompt is similar to the one in Chapter 3, instead of taking a win or lose viewpoint in this prompt, you can look at it from a "money spent" point of view.

Neil Patel of Quicksprout.com is no stranger to creating great products that make money. But not all of his choices are so wise, as you'll learn after reading his "7 Lessons Learned from Losing $739,135 in Bad Investments"[26].

And while your loss (or spending) doesn't have to be that great to make an impact, what matters is what you gained from it, and what lessons you can share with your readers as a result.

The advice could be as simple as truly negotiating a great deal before you waste money, to more common sense measures that still need repeating, such as avoiding putting all your eggs in one basket, or spreading yourself too thin.

Remember, it's not truly a loss if you've gained the wisdom and foresight to share it (even though the financial impact may sting a bit!)

[26] 7 Lessons Learned from Losing $739,135 in Bad Investments
http://www.quicksprout.com/2013/05/13/7-lessons-learned-from-losing-739135-in-bad-investments/

What Was Your Industry Like 10 Years Ago? What Improvements Have Been Made Since Then? What Shouldn't Have Changed?

10 years can seem like a lifetime on the Internet, and for some businesses, technology moves and ideas shift so fast that it can be hard to keep up. Words and phrases like "cloud computing", "big data" and even companies like "Twitter" would sound completely foreign to us in 2004.

In fact, one of the biggest, most earth-shattering announcements to hit the web back then revolved around...

Email.

2004 was the year that Gmail was introduced[27]. And at the time, it was seen as a huge, improbable deal rife with privacy concerns that still ripple into today. Google was known for search back then, and even Gmail's original creator wasn't so sure the idea would fly.

Oh, how far we've come! 425 *million* accounts later, it's hard for many people to envision a life without Gmail.

So what does this have to do with you?

Take a look at your industry – what was it like ten years ago? Talk about the improvements that have been made and the things you wish had stayed the same, and then invite your audience to share their own perspectives.

---

[27] How Gmail Happened: The Inside Story of its Launch 10 Years Ago
http://time.com/43263/gmail-10th-anniversary/

What New Laws or Changes in Your Industry Go Into Effect this Year?

Laws, bills and acts can have far-reaching implications for almost every business and organization. The good news is, you don't have to be a lawyer to report on these upcoming changes and the effects you foresee them having.

Although this is typically a topic that gets covered around the new year, laws go into effect all the time, so if it's something that looks to have a seismic effect on your industry – there's no time like the present to start talking about it.

Mashable reported on changes that affected the public at the start of 2013, which mean that for "Netflix-loving, drone-fearing, marijuana enthusiast teenagers", life was about to become very different[28].

Although the changes on the horizon don't have to necessarily affect you personally, it's still worth bringing them into the spotlight and encouraging discussion with your readers if you feel that it's a change that could have a major impact on your business or way of life.

[28] 9 Changes to Expect at Midnight on January 1
http://mashable.com/2013/12/31/new-year-changes/

The Origin of _____

There are some unusual origin stories out there. From the use of "OK" to Halloween, the family unit to the dollar sign, there are as many theories and urban legends as there are actual histories.

Even the everyday use of the @ sign in your email has its own accidental history[29].

Dig through a bit of history in your particular topic. Specific jargon, methods and strategies may all have their origins in unusual, exotic and sometimes baffling places. Before you know it, you may uncover a fascinating story that's worth sharing with your readers.

For example, why do we have an eight hour workday? Where did "spelling bees" come from? Whatever your chosen blog subject, giving a bit of insight about the past can serve as entertainment, and a bit of education too.

And that @ sign? It turns out it was haphazardly chosen as a way to identify and send a message from one user at one computer to another, when programmers were building ARPANet – the precursor to today's internet.

---

[29] The Accidental History of the @ Sign
http://www.smithsonianmag.com/science-nature/the-accidental-history-of-the-symbol-18054936/

X Ways to Sabotage Your _____

Everyone wants to pursue their dreams with equal parts gusto and motivation. But as a newcomer to any hobby or task, sometimes you can accidentally do things that will wreck your foundation before you ever start building it.

Most of the time, we make these mistakes and learn from them. Some people, however, like the students that one photographer at Digital Photography School worked with, had big goals, but they were doing everything in their power to make sure their professional efforts never got off the ground.

Read the full list here:

Top 10 Ways to Sabotage Your Professional Photography Aspirations

http://digital-photography-school.com/top-10-ways-to-sabotage-your-professional-photography-aspirations

Some things in the list are common sense, like only showing photos to family and friends, or building a website that makes it impossible to order. Others have more far-reaching implications, like treating ethics as an inconvenience, or just taking photos instead of telling stories.

What steps might your readers be guilty of that are causing them to inadvertently sabotage their dreams and goals as they relate to your topic? Sometimes, a little gentle career advice is all that's needed to get them back on the right track!

The Perks of Having a _____

Do you have access to something that's viewed as rare or valuable by your audience? Even if it's not a material thing per se, giving your readers insight into the benefits of doing or having something unique lets them share that experience with you vicariously.

Sometimes, the thing in question can be viewed as a luxury, such as "The Perks of Having a Personal Shopper[30]". Other times, it can be a side benefit of technology, like "The Perks of Having a Private Netflix Account[31]"

Whatever the perk is, sharing the benefits will give your users a glimpse into your life or workflow in a way that they wouldn't otherwise get. This sort of "insider access" can help you forge new connections as well as answer common questions about the perks you're highlighting.

[30] The Perks of Having a Personal Shopper
http://barbarakingstyling.com/my-blog/143-the-perks-of-having-a-personal-shopper.html

[31] The Perks of Having a Private Netflix Account
mashable.com/2014/07/30/netflix-mashable-minute/

X Things You're Not Doing With Your _____ (That You Should!)

Knowing your topic of interest or industry well also means understanding the little things that most people forget about. Whether you're writing a blog on travel or gardening, listing these little "life hacks" can make life easier for your readers.

For example, did you know that most mobile clicks in an email are actually mistakes? And that there's a single line of text that you can put in your mobile email messages that can improve readability considerably? Those are just a few of the things you'll learn when reading "3 Things You're Not Doing with Your Emails that You Should Start Doing Today[32]" by marketer Jamie Turner.

What are some little known things that you can share with your readers that will improve their lives in some way after reading your post?

[32] 3 Things You're Not Doing with Your Emails that You Should Start Doing Today
http://60secondmarketer.com/blog/2014/01/02/email-marketing-techniques/

The Do's and Don'ts of _____

Just because something is common practice, doesn't mean that it's right (or always has been right). Take the common cold or the flu for example. Everyone has their own special "home remedy" that could end up doing more harm than good.

Many people don't know, for instance, that they should avoid cold medicines when taking the flu and that light to moderate exercise while suffering from a cold can actually make you get over it faster[33].

It's time for you to set the record straight and provide a list of do's and don'ts to your fellow readers. Who knows, you might upset age-old practices and change someone's perspective in the process! At the very least, you'll remind people of the best practices in your particular industry, while showing them how to get the most out of the product or service you provide.

[33] The Do's and Don'ts of Colds and Flu
http://www.dietsinreview.com/diet_column/01/the-dos-and-donts-of-colds-and-the-flu/

Avoid Buying These X Items

For someone just starting out in your niche or industry, it can be tempting to buy the very best. Most likely, they're on a tight budget though, so they have to scrutinize every purchase. Why not help them out?

There are plenty of lists out there on what you *should* buy...are there things you wish you had *not* bought when you first started along your current path? For instance, when outfitting your student's dorm for fall, it's commonplace to want to make major purchases such as printers, a high-end laptop, new clothes and such.

But as this article[34] from Seattle Pi shows us, not all of those purchases are the best use of your (or your student's) money. An iPhone is almost always on the want list, and Apple smartly releases them right around the back-to-school rush. But when they do, the current generation falls in price, making the very latest and greatest model unnecessary.

What are some items your readers should avoid buying if they're looking to break into or improve themselves in your particular field?

[34] Avoid Buying These 10 Items for the College Students in Your Family
http://blog.seattlepi.com/boomerconsumer/2014/08/15/avoid-buying-these-10-items-for-the-college-students-in-your-family/

A Recipe for _____

Unfortunately, your blog may not be the best place for your killer lemon merengue pie, but you can still post a recipe of a different sort.

How would you create a recipe for something intangible, like an epic photo shoot? Photographer Scott Kelby of Photoshop Insider has just the solution[35]. With only three "ingredients", Scott is able to make the entire process look point-and-shoot simple, with breathtaking photos to match.

Could you come up with a recipe for great customer service? What about a recipe for a memorable family outing? Whatever your topic, chances are you can brainstorm some great ideas that are easy to implement and require few ingredients – just a dash of expertise and a hint of determination.

[35] A Recipe for Creating an Epic Looking Shot
http://scottkelby.com/2014/a-recipe-for-creating-an-epic-looking-shot/

Chapter 5: Changes and Shifts

Some of the most consistently popular blog posts don't need much writing from you at all, but rather they shift control into your readers' hands or otherwise question the normal balance and routine of things.

Just because something has "always been done that way", doesn't mean it's the best or most productive way to do it. With that in mind, these posts question the order and evolution of things and get people thinking, "why not?"

Be prepared to face some opposition from those readers who still insist that it's "their way or the highway". These posts aren't meant to provoke or start an argument. Rather, they're designed to give a fresh new perspective on what could be viewed as an outdated, cumbersome or common method.

By adding your own perspective to these prompts, you'll create some great discussions while enlightening your readers to potential changes that could benefit them in the long run.

Become a Better _____: X Habits to Avoid

Nearly everyone wants to improve their situation in life. From reading self-help books to taking workshops to enrolling in conferences, we all view ourselves as imperfect or lacking in some way.

What differs is our beliefs on how things should be handled. From spanking kids vs. time-outs, multitasking vs. concentrating on one task at a time, what you look at as something to be avoided may be another person's proven method.

In one example from Mashable[1], the author lists the traits necessary to become a better boss. Most anyone in a management position would agree that there's a fine line between leading your team and listening to them or giving too much versus giving too little information for your employees to work with.

Where things shift, however, is on what constitutes a "habit" to "avoid". Is doing anything within your power to make your clients happy a trait worth embracing or avoiding? As you'll see, any habit can be taken too far – to the point of being detrimental to one's work.

What are your suggestions on how to become better at what you do? Are there specific habits that you'd advocate avoiding? Why or why not? What do your readers think? If you're not sure, ask them!

[1] Become a Better Boss: 5 Habits Managers Should Avoid
http://mashable.com/2014/07/22/making-employees-lives-hard/

Getting Beyond the _____

Just because things have always been done a certain way, doesn't mean that's the best way, or even the only way to do them. Oftentimes, we feel so stuck and helpless that it's hard to see beyond that – but that's exactly what this prompt is about.

One writer, Scott Anthony, was asking himself the tough questions… on what life might be like in the year 2050[2]. How would we deal with income inequality? What about accessible and affordable healthcare? Or even more importantly, feeding the swelling population of 10 BILLION people?

They're the kinds of questions that scientists, economists and engineers struggle to figure out every day – and yet Scott had an idea that would be worth considering. What if we went beyond the narcissistic state of advertising, and created a worthwhile award for entrepreneurs that innovate and come up with creative solutions that benefit the world as a whole?

What if investors judged their investments based on how much the company put into its own innovation rather than blindly following whatever hot trend is out there?

It makes you think, and even if your blog isn't tackling the hard questions, what's a creative way to go beyond the "stuckness" of a current issue that's plaguing your industry or otherwise hogging all the attention? Can you step up and lead your readers out of the mire of trendiness?

[2] Getting Beyond the Narcissism Advertising Complex
http://blogs.hbr.org/2013/12/getting-beyond-the-narcissismadvertising-complex/

Why X Must Come Before Y

Jolt your readers out of their "regular" way of doing things with this blog prompt. Doing things in a certain order can feel monotonous, but shaking things up a bit can provide a new point of view.

Duct Tape Marketing publisher John Jantsch explained this very concept in a podcast where he was asked to help a medium-sized business formulate a marketing plan – the result of which birthed the article "Why Audience Development Must Come Before Business Development[3]."

It's all too common for businesses to get their message, their brand and their marketing nailed down before looking at a broad swath of an audience and saying "Okay, which one of these groups should we target first?" In all actuality, the process should be reversed – find the people first, and then build the brand around their wants and needs.

What are some points in your industry that people often do in the "wrong" order? Why should one come before the other? Shake up and shift their perspective!

[3] Why Audience Development Must Come Before Business Development
http://www.ducttapemarketing.com/blog/2013/12/11/earning-audience/

Forget Everything You Learned About _____, and Do *This* Instead

Your blog readers, particularly if they follow your industry closely or are in the same line of work, likely have their own processes and methods for doing things.

So with this prompt, you're going to shake up their foundations a bit and force them to start from a blank slate all over again.

What are some points that you wish your readers could completely forget about, and start over with a fresh new perspective or strategy?

The 60 Second Marketer wrote just such a piece, called "Forget Everything You've Learned About SEO [Search Engine Optimization] and Do This One Thing Instead.[4]"

Of course, the "one thing" presented can often come as a shock to your readers – you're essentially telling them to wipe the slate clean and forge a new path instead.

What's something in your subject area of expertise that you'd like your readers to start over fresh with? What knowledge would you share with them that could change their preconceived notions of your topic?

[4] Forget Everything you've Learned About SEO and Do This One Thing Instead
http://60secondmarketer.com/blog/2013/12/12/new-rules-of-seo/

How _____ Can Set You Back

Sometimes, what you view as a positive (say, analysing a certain situation to make sure you know everything you can before you jump in), can actually cause you more trouble in the end.

Such a thing happened to self-improvement expert Shaun Rosenberg, who, in his article entitled, "How Overthinking Can Set You Back[5]", demonstrates that analysis paralysis can lead to a lot of missed opportunities – and what to do about it.

But this prompt doesn't have to be solely about improving oneself. A timely article about the ever-growing and all-important Back to School lists for kids can set parents back hundreds of dollars. Multiply that by the number of kids in a household, and it starts to get ridiculous.

Products, services, software – all of it is fair game for exposing the burden it can take on your health, your finances and beyond. You can also take this post one step further and tell your users how they can get back on track by making a few simple changes.

---

[5] How Overthinking Things Can Set You Back
http://www.shaunrosenberg.com/how-overthinking-things-can-set-you-back

Why X is More Important than Y

This is another statement post that changes places with the commonly-held order or belief of things and then makes a case for its higher importance. For instance:

- Why the Fitness Habit is More Important than the Plan
  https://plus.google.com/+LeoBabauta/posts/G7k6uG5Sryj

- Intelligence Quotient (IQ) or Emotional Quotient (EQ) – Which One is More Important?
  http://psychology.about.com/od/intelligence/fl/IQ-or-EQ-Which-One-Is-More-Important.htm

- Why Your Last Love is More Important than Your First Love
  http://www.huffingtonpost.com/ashley-massis/why-your-last-love-is-more-important-than-your-first-love_b_5697736.html

- Why Customer Retention is More Important than Acquisition
  http://mashable.com/2014/07/22/customer-retention-acquisition/

When making your statement, ask yourself – what things get prioritized and why? How does it change your outlook or results? Although your first few steps into this shift might be a bit wobbly, it's nevertheless worth exploring. Will your readers agree with you? You'll have to write the post and see!

Here's What Happens When...

Your life or your work may seem ordinary to you, but to someone else, it could start a remarkable chain reaction of insights, reflection, and even amusement.

For instance, what would happen if scientists learned how to turn solar wind data into sound[6]? What happens if you give a bunch of adults Play-Doh®[7]? What about when Justin Bieber follows you on Twitter[8]?

Fortunately, you no longer have to wonder. Your fellow bloggers have revealed the answers. Although you might not be an engineer or "worthy" of a follow from "The Biebs", remember that no one else has experienced your life, developed your perspective or come from your background.

Do a little experiment or share the results of an event. Your readers will be entertained, enlightened and engaged – guaranteed.

[6]Here's What Happens When Scientists Turn Solar Wind Data into Sound
http://www.huffingtonpost.com/2014/09/10/solar-wind-sound-nasa-video_n_5791452.html

[7]Here's What Happens When You Give a Bunch of Adults Play-Doh®
http://www.buzzfeed.com/alannaokun/heres-what-happens-when-you-give-play-doh-to-a-bunch-of-adul#1gwqm7a

8 Here's What Happens When Justin Bieber Follows You on Twitter
http://mashable.com/2014/04/24/justin-bieber-twitter-follow/

Let's Do Something About _____

This prompt is your "get-up-and-go" – your voice to rally the masses. Even though you may not feel like you can make a difference, your writing can get the word out and shine the spotlight on what you feel is a problem that's unaddressed, and possibly getting worse.

Take, for example, teenage stress. According to the American Psychological Association, teens are more stressed than their parents[9] – worried about common teenage things like school and getting into a good college, but also surprisingly about things like their parents' finances.

Teens being stressed is nothing new – but what was perhaps most surprising was that they felt the stress wasn't impacting their physical or mental health, when it most certainly was. Let's face it, teenagers don't always get the most sleep or eat well, and all of those issues rolled up together can have a dramatic effect on their lives.

It may seem like a problem that's small and insignificant compared with the other woes and troubles of the world – but it's also an issue that people don't feel is too large for them to handle.

What is something you'd like to bring more attention to in your own field or specialty? How can your readers lend a hand?

[9] Let's Do Something About Teen Stress
http://www.kevinmd.com/blog/2014/03/lets-teen-stress.html

How X is Leading the Way on (Topic)

Another prompt for shifts or changes is to focus the microscope on leaders; in particular, leaders that tackle the hard issues and talk about the topics that people care about.

Retirement is one such issue. Some people are nearing retirement age but aren't quite ready to quit working just yet. They may not be as financially stable as they thought, but there are also some nagging health concerns and time with family to consider.

That's why Washington has started to gradually introduce the concept of phased retirement[10]. Although employers haven't shown much interest, employees are excited about the prospect and would welcome its implementation, according to a recent study.

What are some ways that you can profile leaders or start-ups in your industry who are blazing a trail on a topic that may be hard to talk about, or a problem that seems too overwhelming to try and solve?

[10] How Washington is Leading the Way on Phased Retirement
http://retirementrevised.com/how-washington-is-leading-the-way-on-phased-retirement/

How to Upgrade Your _____

Sometimes in life, we need an upgrade -- maybe not a complete overhaul, but a little jolt toward the latest and greatest version. The good news is that upgrades aren't just limited to computers. You can upgrade your wardrobe, your kitchen, and even your resume[11].

But even once you know you need an upgrade, how do you go about it? Go through the process step by step for your readers.

In some cases, such as the aforementioned resume upgrade, the topic itself may be too large to tackle all at once. If that's the case, follow their example and break your post up into several sections. Let your readers know that an upgrade doesn't have to be a huge, expensive, time consuming task, but can be done with smaller steps over time.

By breaking down each step into its approximate timeframe and/or budget (if needed), you'll make the task much more manageable for your readers and show them that 'hey! I really can do that!"

[11] How to Upgrade Your Resume
http://www.personalbrandingblog.com/how-to-upgrade-your-resume-part-1/

The Major Element Missing From _____

Have you ever watched or listened to something and thought "something's missing…" This is your chance to tell your readers exactly what that something is.

Fans of the original Guardians of the Galaxy comic were no doubt disappointed when the main protagonist Peter Quill / Star Lord was seen without his signature sidearm, the Element Gun[12]. What's more, you could go into some detail or speculation on *why* the thing was missing, or when/if it might be brought back.

And your revelation doesn't have to revolve around movies, TV shows or books. In another example, the author explores pieces that are missing from your business continuity plan[13]. What are some pieces you feel are missing from companies, events or other happenings in your industry? Share these on your blog and invite your readers to share their perspective.

[12] The Major Element Missing from Guardians of the Galaxy
http://mashable.com/2014/08/04/element-gun-guardians-of-the-galaxy-peter-quill-star-lord/

[13] 3 Important Elements Your Business Continuity Plan is Missing
http://www.forbes.com/sites/sungardas/2014/08/13/3-important-elements-your-business-continuity-plan-is-missing/

X Decisions that Shaped the _____ Industry

Back in the late 1990s and early 2000s, no one could have ever guessed that MP3s would overtake CDs, or that Apple would become an iconic innovator whose pivotal release of the iPod in 2001 almost didn't happen[14].

Even when production was about to start, there were still major glitches to overcome, including one which caused the batteries to drain even when the device was off, resulting in just a 3 hour battery life.

The fixes, including Steve Jobs' daily involvement in the conceptualization and finalization of the product, likely helped shape Apple's dominance for years to come.   And that's just one example.

Another involves celebrities and how their decisions shape our healthcare choices[15]. For instance, Angelina Jolie went through a preventive double mastectomy because of her genetic predisposition to breast cancer. Other people may also be predisposed to breast cancer, but to them, such a life-changing decision seems smart because a celebrity did it.

You may need to do a bit of digging to find the game-changing points in your industry where corporate shifts or popular opinion caused major underlying changes. Share these with your readers and think about what life could be like if those changes were never made? Do you feel that the changes improved your business or niche for better or worse?

[14] Inside Look at Birth of the iPod
http://archive.wired.com/gadgets/mac/news/2004/07/64286?currentPage=all

[15] How Celebrities Shape Our Healthcare Decisions
http://www.fiercehealthcare.com/story/how-celebrities-shape-our-healthcare-decisions-good-or-ill/2013-12-19?page=full

What's *Really* Missing From Your _____?

Whether it's your life, your vacation or your kids' school lunches, sometimes you feel like something's missing – you're just not sure what. In the case of photographer Olivier Duong, he felt his photos were incredible – ready to be crowned and shown off as the perfect examples of composition that they were.

Except there was something missing... something intangible. Olivier could see it in others' photos, and it took a terrible tragedy for him to discover it for himself[16].

While your "something missing" doesn't have to involve such a tragedy, nor cause a crisis to be discovered, its job is nevertheless to make the connection that many readers didn't know existed.

Whether it's a product or a more intangible "something" is completely up to you to find and share.

[16] What's Really Missing from Your Photographs?
http://digital-photography-school.com/whats-really-missing-photographs/

Why We _____

It sounds simple enough, but sometimes even the simplest statement can have profound psychological roots that plunge deep into the heart of what makes us unique.

For example, when it comes to sharing a controversial or unpopular point of view, do you find yourself deleting that Facebook or Twitter status before you even finish it? You're not alone – and ReadWrite, as well as a Pew study, back up the findings – we tend to self-censor on social media[17].

Another article from the same site that came at an opportune time, especially considering the privacy issues with the Facebook messaging app promotes the point of view of Why We Need Messaging Apps.[18]

Go ahead and take a stand and delve a bit deeper into why we do the things we do. Is there something controversial about your industry that we need or should try to better understand before making a judgment for or against it?

[17] Why We Self-Censor on Social Media
http://readwrite.com/2014/08/27/pew-proves-we-hate

[18] Why We Need Messaging Apps
http://readwrite.com/2014/08/26/messaging-authenticity-social-media

Types of People at (Event or Type of Business)

If you're new to a certain event, conference or culture, chances are you'll meet some pretty…interesting individuals. Don't you wish there were a sort of survival guide to browse before you go? That's precisely what this post is about.

What kind of people can one expect to meet in your particular niche or topic area? If you go to conferences surrounding your business or industry, what type of individuals might people be meeting there?

Of course, it's impossible to pigeon-hole people into small, compartmentalized boxes based on a handful of traits, but knowing what to expect beforehand can make all the difference in getting to know someone and why they act or react the way they do.

It may be a bit tongue-in-cheek stereotypical, but deep down, there's a grain of truth to the perception, such as:

The 24 Types of People at Startups
http://www.popsugar.com/tech/Types-People-Start-Ups-35170430

17 People You Meet at Every Hostel
http://blog.wehostels.com/people-at-every-hostel/

The 12 Types of People You'll Meet at a Conference
http://blog.hubspot.com/marketing/types-of-people-at-conferences

What are some of the personality types one is likely to run into in your line of work?

Need to (Goal)? There's an App for That®

One of the original (and still one of the biggest) selling points of the Apple iPhone was that "there's an app for that." In fact, the phrase has become so commonplace with smart phones and related devices that Apple smartly trademarked it.

In reality, there are apps for virtually every want and need on the market. You can manage water savings through the latest in drought technology[19], choose a great watermelon or even try Snapchat for cats ("Snapcat")[20]

Browsing the App Store or Android App Marketplace will give you an app for nearly anything – so why not highlight a few on your blog and invite your readers to share a few of your favorites? Better yet, if you can tie it in to achieving a goal such as conquering insomnia[21], you can motivate your readers to finally take action toward overcoming something they may have previously found too daunting.

[19] The California Drought: There's an App for That
http://spectrum.ieee.org/view-from-the-valley/consumer-electronics/gadgets/the-california-drought-theres-an-app-for-that

[20] 10 Oddest Apps in the World Today
http://www.techradar.com/us/news/phone-and-communications/there-s-an-app-for-that-10-oddest-apps-in-the-world-today-1184570#null

[21] Conquer Insomnia in 6 Weeks? There's an App for That and It Could Change Your Life
http://www.fastcompany.com/3035687/healthware/from-insomniac-to-deep-sleeper-in-six-weeks-theres-an-app-for-that-and-it-could-c

Is Your _____ Damaging Your _____?

Sometimes, the products we use or the routines we find ourselves in every day can inadvertently damage our health or productivity. Here's your chance to highlight these problems on your blog, and give your users ways to overcome them.

From the simple "Are computer screens damaging your eyes[22]?" to the more complex, "Are your internal systems damaging your business"[23]?" there's no shortage of topics that can merit extra attention on your blog.

Once you've highlighted the problem, discuss the issues that can cause it, as well as potential remedies (though it's usually never that simple). Oftentimes, simply becoming aware of the problem is enough to make people want to take steps to overcome it – so sharing those points may be the extra nudge they need to act.

[22] Are Computer Screens Damaging Your Eyes?
http://www.cnn.com/2013/11/12/health/upwave-computer-eyes/

[23] Are Your Internal Systems Damaging Your Business?
http://www.smashingmagazine.com/2014/09/12/are-your-internal-systems-damaging-your-business/

(Event/Product/Experiment) Will Make You Rethink (Topic)

If you consider yourself a Twitter power user, you likely saw some changes in August of 2014 that made you pause – Twitter was suddenly mentioning your followers' favorites in your timeline as if they were retweets[24].

Think of the implications of that for a second. If you maintain a well-groomed, meticulously managed Twitter feed (and many people do), suddenly seeing other people's favorites is cause for alarm. Twitter had purposefully done this in an attempt to encourage more "new eggs" to discover content they liked, but many users took to the social stream to voice their discontent.

It's one thing to favourite something on Twitter. A move that likely will only hold significance for you. However, a retweet is meant to be broadcast from your account to your followers. It's intentional and planned.

With this in mind, are there specific events, products or even experiments in your industry that would cause your readers to want to rethink how they use or participate in them? Divulge all the details on your blog and why your readers should be cautious or even excited about the change.

---

[24] Twitter's Retweet Experiment Will Make You Rethink Your Favorites
http://readwrite.com/2014/08/18/twitter-experiment-retweet-favorites-timeline

Tricks Every (Type of Person) Should Know

Although this prompt technically doesn't cover a change or shift, it can cause those very things to happen for your readers. For instance, we all know someone who we can say with absolute certainty is not a "morning person".

Thankfully, entertainment site Buzzfeed has outlined a few small "hacks" and tricks that every night owl should know to make those mornings a bit more survivable[25]. Although light-hearted, the suggestions will nevertheless make you stop and think, "Wow, I never knew they invented that!"

From alarm clocks you have to chase (or shoot) to a gadget that works with your body's natural sleep rhythms, there are plenty of short, workable tips that even the most sleep-starved zombie can appreciate.

What are some little-known or under-utilized tips or tricks in your industry that your readers can use to make the most out of your product or service?

[25] 21 Tricks Every Non-Morning Person Should Know
http://www.buzzfeed.com/alannaokun/just-five-more-minutes

Why You Must Not Ignore _____

From a strange pain in an unusual place[26], to the call for adventure[27], there are some things you simply should not ignore. Although your particular focus may not be a life-or-death matter, it could cause your readers some regret or uncertainty if they choose not to pay attention to it.

In bringing a topic to light, you not only give your readers the opportunity to (re)discover it, but you also place significant importance on the task – thereby making them aware of it and possibly prompting a change in their own life.

Either way, choosing to highlight the issue often means taking a stand and talking about the very things that have remained hidden all this time. Bring them out. Talk about them with your readers. Make sure they know how to take action should the problem get worse. It may not save a life, but it will make a difference.

[26] 7 Pains You Shouldn't Ignore
http://www.webmd.com/heart-disease/features/7-pains-you-shouldnt-ignore?page=2&rdspk=active

[27] Why You Must Not Ignore the Call to Adventure
http://www.copyblogger.com/pursue-adventure/

Why No One's Going to Win the (Topic) Wars

Whether it's a fight over independence or in-app messaging[28], the battles can be just as decisive as the war itself. With blogging, every controversial post is made with the hope of changing someone else's point of view (or getting more people to agree with yours!)

Unfortunately, this is rarely ever the case, as the people on the opposite end of the spectrum likely have their own reasons for defending or attacking your post, just as you do. And that's exactly what this prompt is about.

But it's not just about the futility of trying to "convert" someone to your way of thinking, or convincing someone to adopt your particular methodology. The roots go much deeper than that.

What happens when different groups splinter off? What happens to people that are caught in the middle – who don't want to "pick a side"? Why does no one ultimately win? What should be done about it, if anything? This is your opportunity to make your position on the matter clear.

[28] Why No One's Going to Win the Messaging Wars
http://readwrite.com/2014/08/13/messaging-apps-fight-texting

The Final Word on Blogging

These blog prompts are meant to give you a spark of inspiration and motivation. Now it's your turn to make them your own. Remember that no one else can write like you, and even the best bloggers have their favorite pieces that truly catapulted them into the annals of success.

The important thing is that the sooner you start, the sooner you'll be able to attract customers, invite discussion, and create a loyal legion of fans.

Be sure to visit blogprompts.com for the latest updates and new prompts to spur your writing forward! Good luck!

About the Author

Sherice Jacob has played an integral role in creating several successful blogs and web businesses – both for herself and others. She maintains a full-service copywriting and conversion optimization agency at iElectrify.com which helps to improve sales funnels, increase customer retention and improve overall brand awareness.

Sherice currently lives in Charleston, West Virginia and enjoys living life to the fullest together with her husband, Timo.